P9-DFA-642

"We are fighting a bigger fight."

HERA SYNDULLA

STAR WARS REBELS™

VISUAL GUIDE

EPIC BATTLES

**WRITTEN BY
ADAM BRAY**

CONTENTS

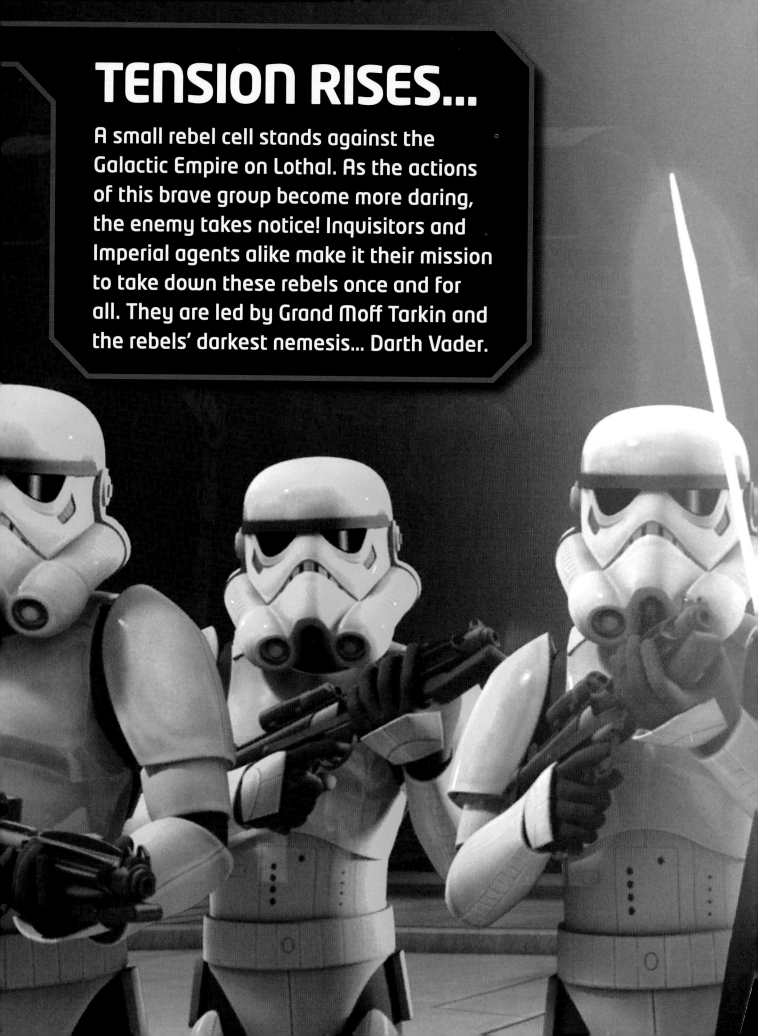

TENSION RISES...

A small rebel cell stands against the Galactic Empire on Lothal. As the actions of this brave group become more daring, the enemy takes notice! Inquisitors and Imperial agents alike make it their mission to take down these rebels once and for all. They are led by Grand Moff Tarkin and the rebels' darkest nemesis... Darth Vader.

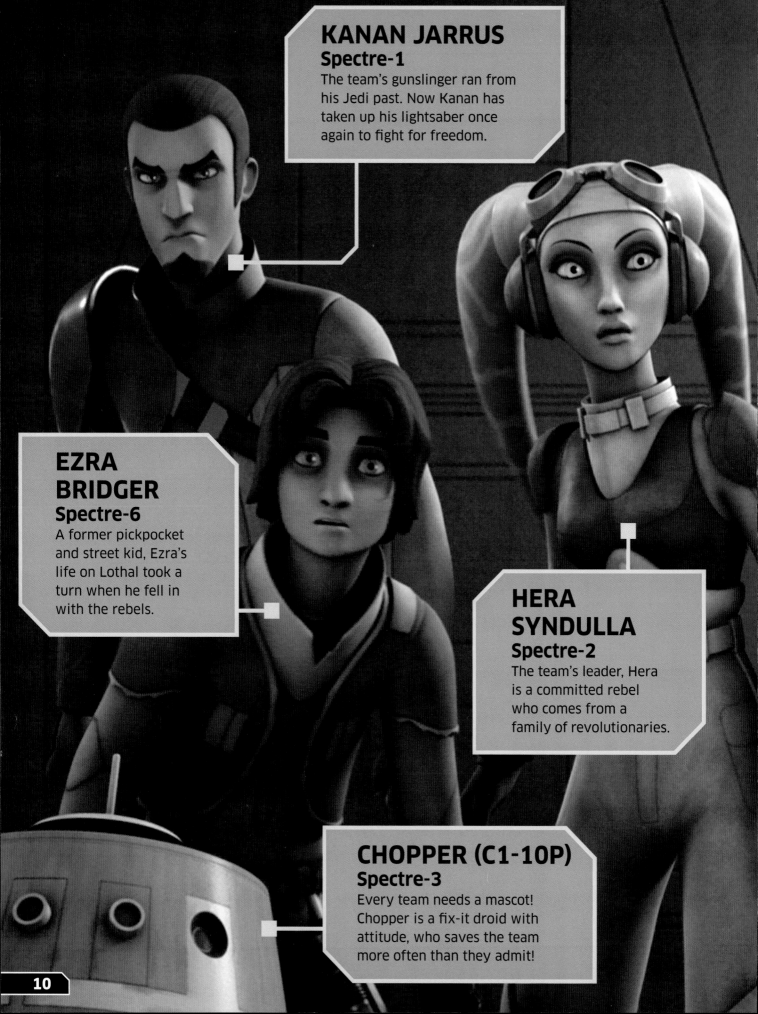

KANAN JARRUS
Spectre-1
The team's gunslinger ran from his Jedi past. Now Kanan has taken up his lightsaber once again to fight for freedom.

EZRA BRIDGER
Spectre-6
A former pickpocket and street kid, Ezra's life on Lothal took a turn when he fell in with the rebels.

HERA SYNDULLA
Spectre-2
The team's leader, Hera is a committed rebel who comes from a family of revolutionaries.

CHOPPER (C1-10P)
Spectre-3
Every team needs a mascot! Chopper is a fix-it droid with attitude, who saves the team more often than they admit!

THE REBELS FIGHT ON

Each of the rebels comes from a very different world. However, they are united in their shared beliefs. The rebels have formed a cell with a common goal—to resist the Empire and aid helpless fellow citizens who suffer under oppressive Imperial rule!

ZEB ORRELIOS
Spectre-4
The team's muscle isn't just a big brute! Zeb is an intelligent, sensitive Lasat who looks out for the weak.

SABINE WREN
Spectre-5
Resourceful Sabine is the group's Mandalorian weapons expert. Her past with the Empire motivates her rebel fight.

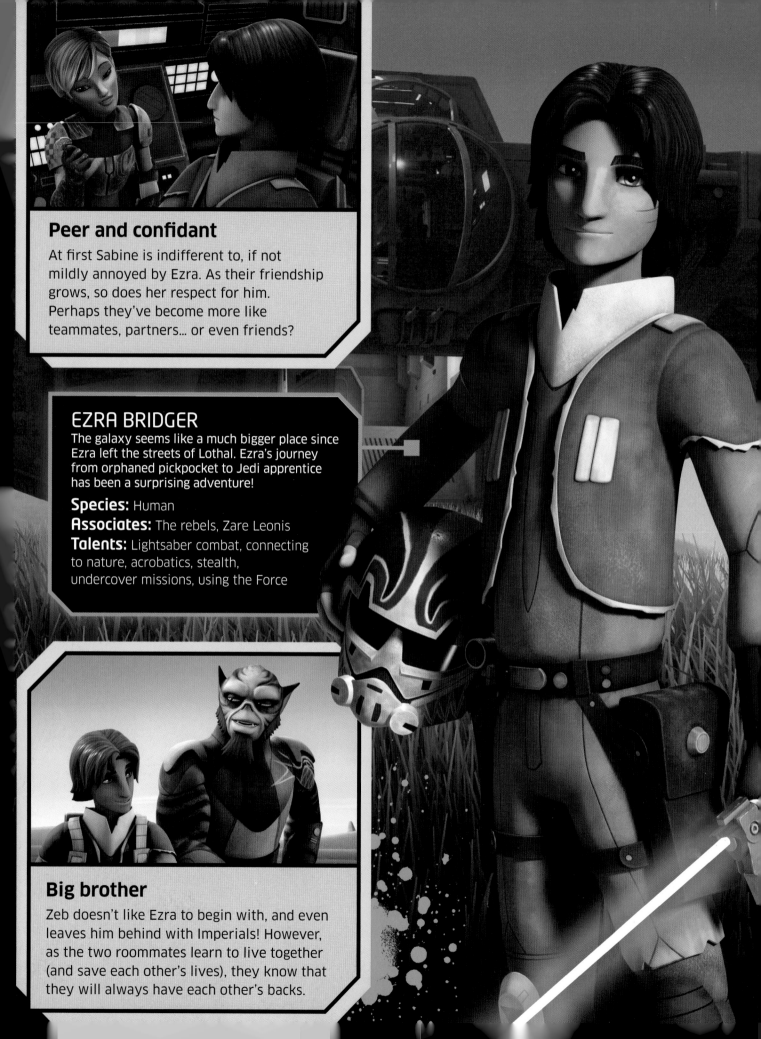

Peer and confidant

At first Sabine is indifferent to, if not mildly annoyed by Ezra. As their friendship grows, so does her respect for him. Perhaps they've become more like teammates, partners... or even friends?

EZRA BRIDGER

The galaxy seems like a much bigger place since Ezra left the streets of Lothal. Ezra's journey from orphaned pickpocket to Jedi apprentice has been a surprising adventure!

Species: Human

Associates: The rebels, Zare Leonis

Talents: Lightsaber combat, connecting to nature, acrobatics, stealth, undercover missions, using the Force

Big brother

Zeb doesn't like Ezra to begin with, and even leaves him behind with Imperials! However, as the two roommates learn to live together (and save each other's lives), they know that they will always have each other's backs.

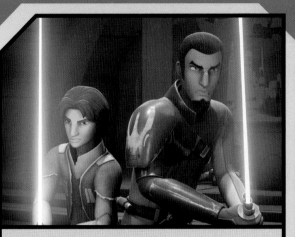

Guardian mentor

Kanan initially doubted his ability to teach Ezra, but now Master and Padawan work well together. Kanan is very protective of Ezra, but also very proud of his progress as a Jedi.

Maternal team leader

It was Hera's idea for Kanan to recruit Ezra and train him as a Jedi. She and Ezra may not always agree on everything, but Hera always puts the team first and has Ezra's best interests in mind.

ONE OF THE TEAM

Since joining the crew of the *Ghost* and becoming a rebel, Ezra has found a new family and a new purpose in life. Like most teenagers, he does question his role in the team sometimes, but in the end he knows that when he found the rebels, he found his home.

Mechanical buddy

Apart from Hera, Ezra is the only other member of the crew who takes the time to listen to what Chopper is saying. The two may prank each other and even fight sometimes, but they have a strong bond and understand each other very well.

Sheev Palpatine rules the Galactic Empire from Coruscant. He is also secretly the Sith Lord, Darth Sidious.

Emperor

Darth Vader is the Sith apprentice of the Emperor. Except for Tarkin, Vader commands all of the Emperor's servants.

Sith Lord

Grand Moffs are governors of "priority sectors." These are usually regions with many planetary systems.

Grand Moffs

The Inquisitors are appointed by Darth Vader and command the Imperial military. Their purpose is to hunt Jedi.

Inquisitors

Imperial Security Bureau (ISB)

The ISB oversees security and loyalty to the Empire. It falls under the Commission for the Preservation of the New Order.

ESCALATION

After Kallus, the Inquisitor, and even Governor Tarkin are unable to capture Lothal's rebels, the Emperor sends an "alternative solution." Palpatine instructs his apprentice, Darth Vader, to crush the rebels and bring back order to the Lothal system.

ORDER OF THE EMPIRE

BLOCKADE

In an effort to capture the rebels, the Empire creates a blockade of Star Destroyers over Lothal. Imperial battleships now monitor all vessels coming or going from the planet. Everyone is being watched!

MINISTRY OF INFORMATION

The Ministry of Information is a division of the Coalition for Progress. It manages the Imperial Press Corps and their courier droids. It also controls all media outlets and events, which are used to promote the Empire and spread lies about the rebels.

Local governors are the top Imperial authorities on planets, but they are tightly controlled by those with more authority.

Officers command the Imperial military's troops. They can move up the ranks to command their own Star Destroyer.

Planetary Governors

Imperial Officers

Stormtroopers, TIE pilots, and other highly trained soldiers maintain order by fighting the Empire's wars.

Imperial Troops

Imperial Cadets

The Empire's power structure is vast and complicated. Those who serve it have many different roles to play, but they share one common goal—to keep control over the galaxy and its citizens at all costs.

Young men and women on multiple worlds enroll in Imperial academies to become the next Imperial troops.

Difficult Padawan

Ezra is upset and hurt when he learns that Kanan was hoping to have another Jedi take over his training. When Kanan explains that he was afraid he wasn't a skilled enough teacher, Ezra reassures him that there is no one else he would rather have as a Master.

GETTING TO GRIPS WITH THE FORCE

Every Jedi must learn to focus their mind, but Ezra is particularly undisciplined for a Padawan his age. He has had a late start to his training, but his powers are strong. As Ezra's abilities grow, Kanan worries about his own ability to teach and protect his student.

The *Ghost's* dorsal CEC dual laser turret

Crate of falumpaset milk canisters

Lightsaber training

Kanan has to keep his Jedi powers a secret, and so he is reluctant to display his lightsaber openly. He teaches Ezra not to use a lightsaber unless absolutely necessary. Nonetheless, it is important for Kanan to help Ezra become a skilled Jedi swordsman.

"Do or do not. There is no try."
KANAN JARRUS

KANAN JARRUS

Caleb Dume went into hiding when his Master was killed on the planet Kaller, following Order 66. He changed his name to Kanan Jarrus and turned his back on his Jedi teachings... until he met Ezra.

Species: Human
Associates: The rebels, Ahsoka Tano, Captain Rex
Talents: Jedi abilities, leadership, racing speeders, marksmanship

Chopper waits to throw canisters at Ezra

Improving abilities

Kanan never completed his own training to become a Jedi Knight. The Jedi Order was shattered when he was still a Padawan, so his own skills are undeveloped. By teaching Ezra, Kanan also learns and matures himself.

THERE IS NO "TRY"

Kanan struggles to pass on ancient Jedi teachings. He realizes that he did not understand them himself until now. In order to succeed, Kanan must teach; not merely try to teach.

GARAZEB ORRELIOS

Zeb is a former member of the Lasan Honor Guard, and one of the last of his kind. The Empire ruined his homeworld. Now Zeb fights to prevent that from happening to others.

Species: Lasat
Associates: The rebels
Talents: Close combat with his fists and bo-rifle, intimidating people

Bunkmates

Sharing a room with someone isn't easy—Zeb and Ezra get on each other's nerves a lot! When their squabbling gets too much, Hera likes to assign them jobs, so that they have to work together.

"Amuse me. Use the Force!"

ZEB ORRELIOS

PEACE FOR THE PRESENT

Shared success can inspire good will—as Ezra discovers when Zeb gives him a TIE helmet as a peace offering.

The Force vs. brute force

Zeb and Ezra have a competitive relationship, as each tries to prove they can out-do the other. Ezra may have the Force, but Zeb is bigger, stronger, and more experienced.

UNLIKELY FRIENDS

When Ezra joins the rebels, Zeb has no desire to work with him—and the feeling is mutual! What could a smelly alien have in common with a human boy? However, the two will have to learn to live together—whether they like it or not!

The TIE that binds

When two very different people share a common experience, it can create a strong bond. Ezra and Zeb grow closer when they steal a TIE fighter together. They realize that when they stop bickering and work together, they actually make a pretty incredible team!

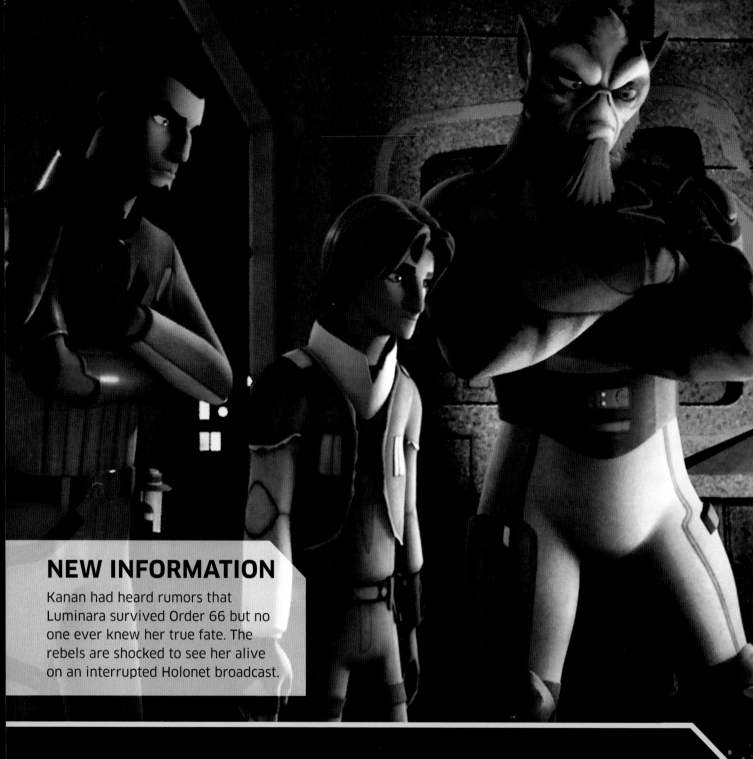

NEW INFORMATION

Kanan had heard rumors that
Luminara survived Order 66 but no
one ever knew her true fate. The
rebels are shocked to see her alive
on an interrupted Holonet broadcast.

THE RESCUE OF LUMINARA UNDULI

Almost all of the Jedi were destroyed when the Emperor issued
Order 66. The rebels learn that Jedi Master Luminara Unduli
survived the attack and is being held prisoner by the Empire in
the Stygeon system. They devise a plan and race to her rescue!

"She was a great Jedi Master."

KANAN JARRUS

Jedi prisoner

The Spire prison is almost impossible to infiltrate, but Kanan and Ezra force their way in, knocking out stormtroopers as they search for Luminara's cell. They find her... or at least they think they do! Something is definitely off.

DID YOU KNOW?

Order 66 occurred during the Battle of Kashyyyk— clone troopers were given an order to turn against their Jedi commanders and kill them all!

It's a trap!

The image of Luminara is revealed to be just a hologram. The Inquisitor has used her bones to lure Kanan into his trap and so far it has worked! The Inquisitor has the Jedi exactly where he wants him.

INQUISITOR STRIKES!

Kanan has never faced a foe as ruthless as the Inquisitor. He and Ezra were unprepared for their surprise encounter, but are able to work together to defend themselves. Nonetheless, they barely escape from the Inquisitor's trap on Stygeon Prime.

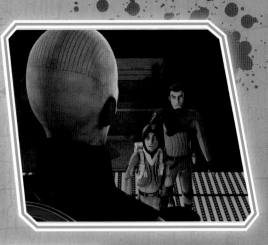

1 The Inquisitor enters the room and draws his lightsaber blade. After introducing himself, he reveals that Luminara Unduli's remains were used to lure Jedi into a trap!

2 When the Inquisitor informs them that their friends will not be coming to their aid, Kanan lunges at him. However, the Jedi is outmatched—the Inquisitor is a superior fighter!

3 Kanan is shocked! Within just a few seconds of dueling, the Inquisitor deduces not only Kanan's fighting style (Form 3, or "Soresu"), but also that his former master was Depa Billaba (who was slain by her own officers in Order 66).

THE INQUISITOR

The Grand Inquisitor leads a secret order, charged by Darth Vader to hunt down remaining Jedi. He uses the Jedi archives on Coruscant to study their traditions and techniques, so he can rapidly identify and destroy his Jedi targets!

Species: Pau'an
Associates: Darth Vader, Agent Kallus, Governor Tarkin
Talents: Using the dark side of the Force, lightsaber dueling, analysis

4 Ezra distracts the Inquisitor and blows the door open with a thermal detonator. The Inquisitor follows Ezra and Kanan as they retreat into the corridor, drawing out his second lightsaber blade.

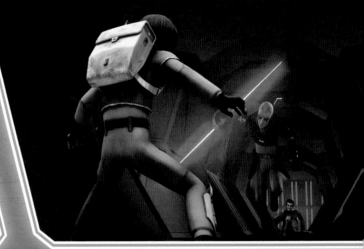

5 The Inquisitor tries to divide Master from Padawan with fear. He taunts Kanan, asking whether he thinks he can really save Ezra, and tells him he should surrender now.

6 The Inquisitor Force-pushes Kanan aside and tells Ezra that his Master is unfocused and undisciplined. Ezra defiantly replies that this makes them perfect for each other.

7 As the Inquisitor advances on Ezra, Kanan desperately uses the Force to slam the Inquisitor against the ceiling. Ezra has just enough time to run to Kanan before the Inquisitor drops to the floor.

8 Kanan and Ezra run through the corridors until they find Zeb and Sabine, and the rebels manage to find a way out of the prison. The furious Inquisitor is close behind them, but they escape on the *Ghost* just in time.

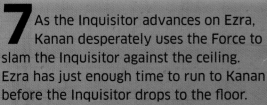

"The Jedi
are dead."
THE INQUISITOR

Battle on Stygeon Prime

The Inquisitor confronts Kanan and Ezra. He believes that he is more than a match for the inexperienced Jedi.

ARTOO VS. CHOPPER

These two droids may have similar designs, but their personalities are entirely different! If Artoo is a pet anooba, then Chopper is a wild Loth-cat. Artoo puts his masters first and never questions his orders. Chopper, however, never stops arguing!

R2-D2 (ARTOO)

Artoo was once the property of the Royal Security Forces of Naboo, stationed on the queen's starship. He served Padmé Amidala and Anakin Skywalker during the Clone Wars, and now serves the House Organa.

Manufacturer: Industrial Automaton

Equipment: Grasping arm, computer probe, booster rockets, scanner antennae, holographic projector, tow cable, arc welder, buzzsaw

Duty above all

Artoo and his partner, C-3PO, go on secret missions for the rebel senator, Bail Organa. Artoo has a gentle, obedient nature and would never dream of pranking Bail or misbehaving like Chopper!

DROID FIGHT!
Chopper starts a fight with R2-D2 to stall the Imperials in the Garel spaceport. This comes easily for Chopper, since he doesn't like other astromechs!

Out for a good time
Chopper enjoys zapping droids and creatures alike with his electroshock prod. He relishes shocking Ezra all the more! Chopper doesn't hold back, even when they are supposed to be just acting. It's too much fun!

C1-10P (CHOPPER)
Chopper is an old and grumpy droid that belongs to Hera, but she considers him part of the crew. He is independent and stubborn, but he cares about his crewmates.

Manufacturer: Unknown
Equipment: Three mechanical arms, computer probe, booster rocket, electroshock prod, circular saw, holographic projector

GRUDGE MATCH

Agent Kallus was there when the Empire destroyed Zeb's homeworld, Lasan. He ordered stormtroopers to wipe out Zeb's fellow Lasats with T-7 ion disrupters. Kallus even stole his signature J-19 bo-rifle from a fallen Lasan Honor Guardsman. Now Zeb wants justice for Kallus' brutality!

DID YOU KNOW?

The EMP generator tips on bo-rifles carry a maximum charge of 11,000 volts. The rifle's plasma gas cartridge packs a powerful punch!

Until the next time...

Their bo-rifles may be similar, but Zeb's fury is no match for Kallus' ISB training. Kallus is easily able to block each of Zeb's angry blows, before delivering a series of deadly electric shocks.

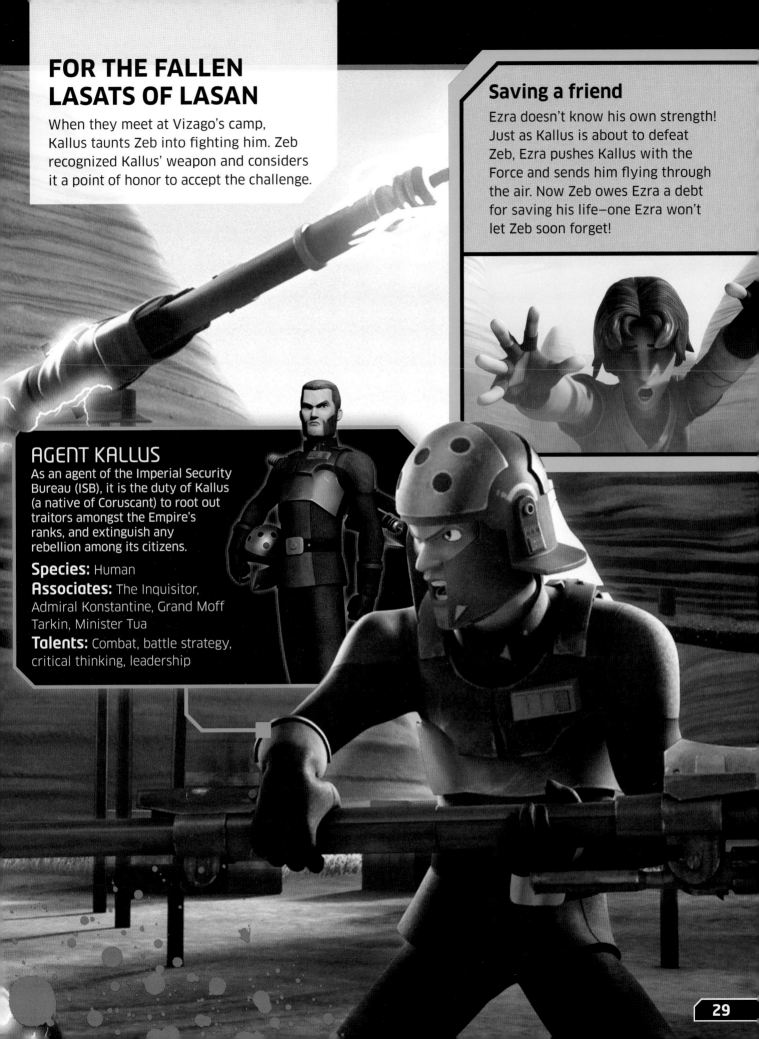

FOR THE FALLEN LASATS OF LASAN

When they meet at Vizago's camp, Kallus taunts Zeb into fighting him. Zeb recognized Kallus' weapon and considers it a point of honor to accept the challenge.

Saving a friend

Ezra doesn't know his own strength! Just as Kallus is about to defeat Zeb, Ezra pushes Kallus with the Force and sends him flying through the air. Now Zeb owes Ezra a debt for saving his life—one Ezra won't let Zeb soon forget!

AGENT KALLUS

As an agent of the Imperial Security Bureau (ISB), it is the duty of Kallus (a native of Coruscant) to root out traitors amongst the Empire's ranks, and extinguish any rebellion among its citizens.

Species: Human

Associates: The Inquisitor, Admiral Konstantine, Grand Moff Tarkin, Minister Tua

Talents: Combat, battle strategy, critical thinking, leadership

MINISTER MAKETH TUA

Maketh Tua is an Imperial government official who manages Lothal's affairs while Governor Arihnda Pryce is on Coruscant. She graduated from the Imperial Academy with honors. Tua is a true patriot, but grows concerned when Tarkin arrives on Lothal.

Ear coverings play Imperial broadcasts.

Armored hat

Protective shoulder plates

Pouch contains data store and secur codes.

SPECIAL EQUIPMENT:
Holdout blaster pistol

SPECIES: Human

AGE: 32

HOMEWORLD: Lothal

Mission to Garel

Maketh accompanies Amda Wabo, an Aqualish arms dealer, to Lothal's sister planet of Garel. However, their deal is thwarted when the rebels steal the Empire's shipment of T-7 disruptors and Tua's borrowed droid assistants, R2-D2 and C-3PO.

Light-weight boots

DATA FILE

PUBLIC PERSONA

Tua enjoys her high Imperial status but she is not evil. She serves the Empire out of a genuine, while misguided, desire to help the citizens of Lothal.

Tua's only hope

Tua is loyal to the Empire, but when Tarkin arrives on Lothal she realizes that she is in danger. She reaches out to the rebels, offering to give them valuable information in return for their help.

Convictions shaken

Tua witnesses the execution of officers Grint and Aresko and is shocked by Grand Moff Tarkin's brutality. When Vader later tells her that she must answer to Tarkin for her failure to capture the rebels, she begins to worry about her own safety.

> "What more does Governor Tarkin expect?"
>
> MINISTER TUA

Moving in

When Governor Tarkin arrives, he takes over Agent Kallus' office. There are other rooms available, but Tarkin's choice sends a strong message: Everyone is in danger of being replaced by someone more capable.

Office lights

DID YOU KNOW?

Many duties in the Imperial Complex are carried out by a variety of droids, including protocol droids, astromechs, mouse droids, and WED treadwells.

IMPERIAL COMPLEX

The Empire maintains a large and imposing headquarters in Lothal's Capital City, which also houses the esteemed Imperial Academy training facility. The complex looms over Lothal, serving as a reminder of Imperial power and control.

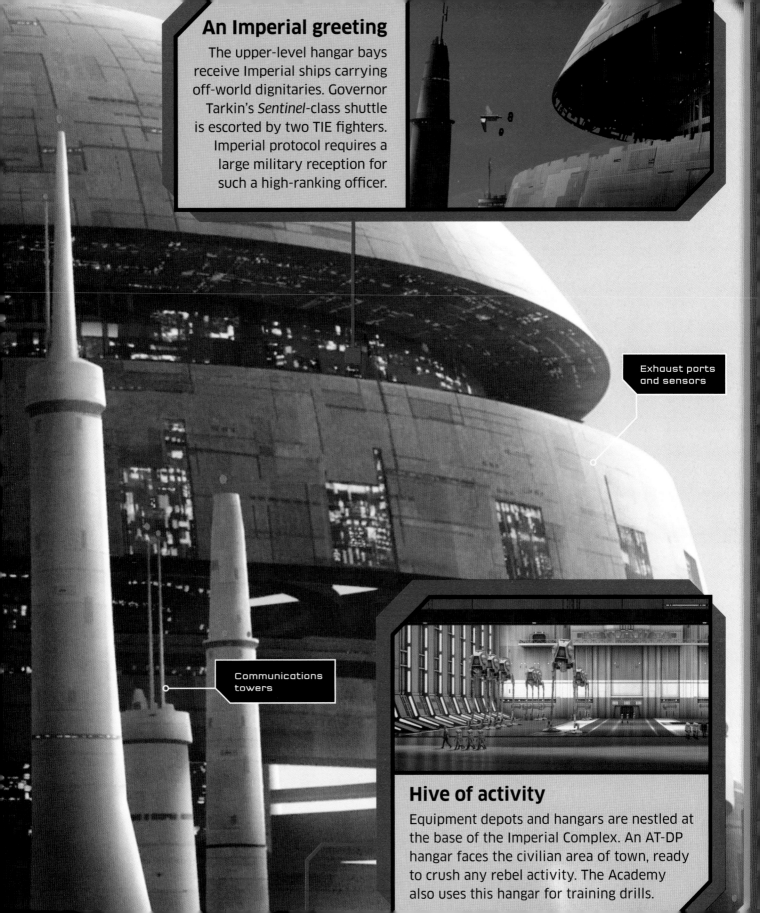

An Imperial greeting

The upper-level hangar bays receive Imperial ships carrying off-world dignitaries. Governor Tarkin's *Sentinel*-class shuttle is escorted by two TIE fighters. Imperial protocol requires a large military reception for such a high-ranking officer.

Exhaust ports and sensors

Communications towers

Hive of activity

Equipment depots and hangars are nestled at the base of the Imperial Complex. An AT-DP hangar faces the civilian area of town, ready to crush any rebel activity. The Academy also uses this hangar for training drills.

Ezra pretends to be a cadet named "Dev Morgan." In order to fit in with the other cadets, he must participate in a series of training exercises led by Commandant Aresko and Taskmaster Grint.

"One decoder, as ordered!"
EZRA BRIDGER

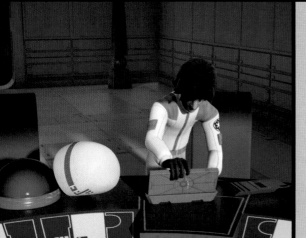

Crunch time

As a cadet, "Dev" can roam freely through Imperial Headquarters. He sneaks into Agent Kallus' office and takes the decoder, but as he leaves, cadet Zare Leonis catches him! Fortunately for Ezra, Zare has his own reason to hate the Empire, and he agrees to help!

EZRA UNDERCOVER

The rebels are determined to destroy a secret Imperial weapons shipment. They have acquired the flight plans for the delivery, but there is a big problem. The coordinates are encrypted! In order to read the data, they must first steal a decoder from Imperial Headquarters in Lothal's capital.

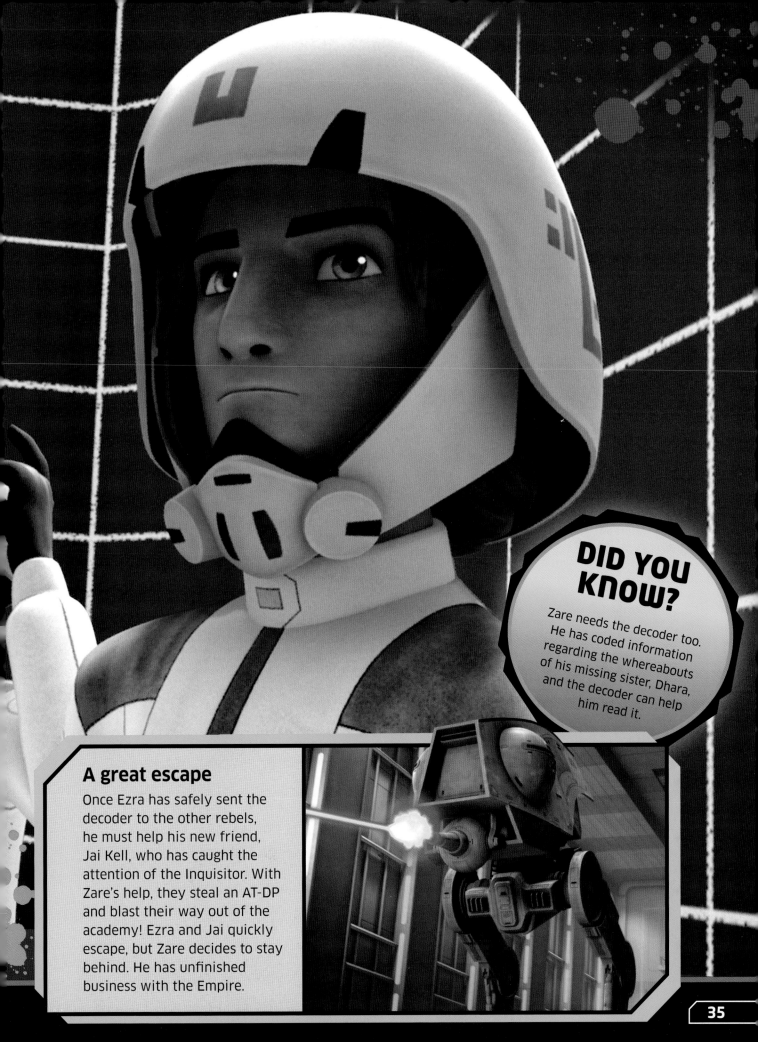

DID YOU KNOW?

Zare needs the decoder too. He has coded information regarding the whereabouts of his missing sister, Dhara, and the decoder can help him read it.

A great escape

Once Ezra has safely sent the decoder to the other rebels, he must help his new friend, Jai Kell, who has caught the attention of the Inquisitor. With Zare's help, they steal an AT-DP and blast their way out of the academy! Ezra and Jai quickly escape, but Zare decides to stay behind. He has unfinished business with the Empire.

Special cadets

The cadets compete in "The Well," jumping on moving platforms as they race to the top. When "Dev" and Jai both set course records during training, it raises Commandant Aresko's suspicions. The Imperial officer believes that the two boys may be Force-sensitive.

DID YOU KNOW?

Ezra replaces a cadet named Pandak Symes when he joins the "Aurek" unit of Imperial Academy squad LRC077.

Reluctant exit

Ezra knows that Jai is in danger now that the Academy has alerted the Inquisitor. He feels obligated to help Jai escape, though Jai is skeptical and frustrated with Ezra's meddling. Jai agrees to leave the Academy because he is worried about his safety; not because he hates the Empire.

ACADEMY CADETS

While he is undercover as "Dev Morgan" at Lothal's Academy for Young Imperials, Ezra makes friends with two cadets named Zare Leonis and Jai Kell. Their fates become intertwined as they make Ezra's mission more complicated than he expected.

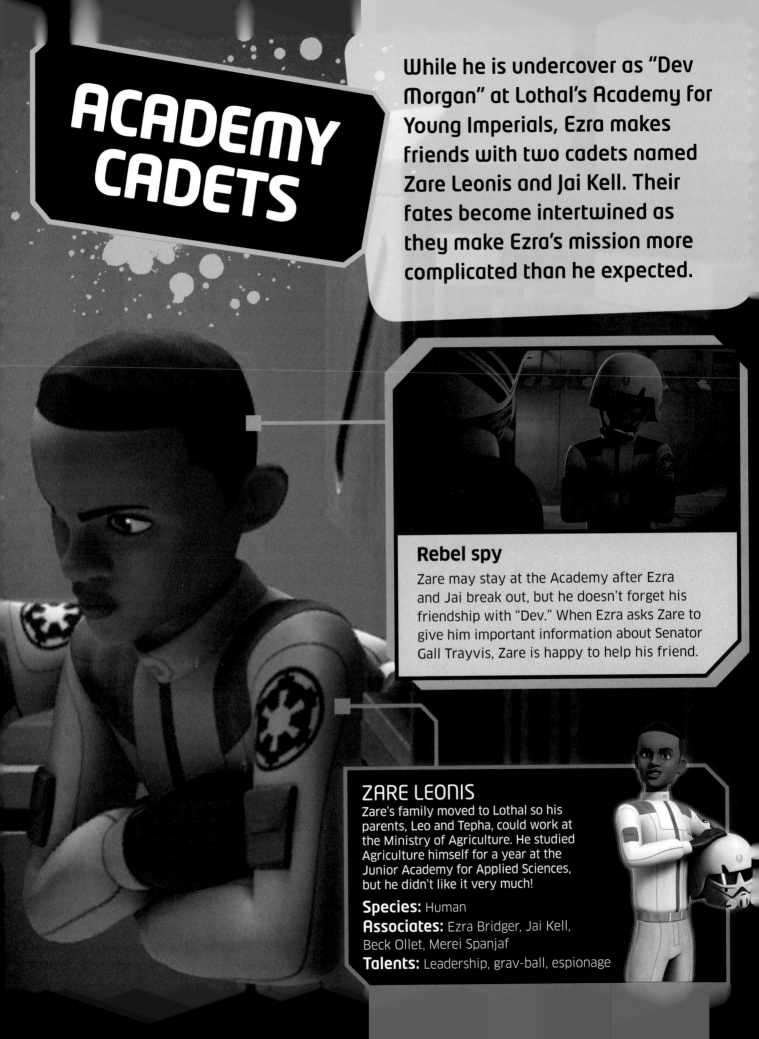

Rebel spy

Zare may stay at the Academy after Ezra and Jai break out, but he doesn't forget his friendship with "Dev." When Ezra asks Zare to give him important information about Senator Gall Trayvis, Zare is happy to help his friend.

ZARE LEONIS

Zare's family moved to Lothal so his parents, Leo and Tepha, could work at the Ministry of Agriculture. He studied Agriculture himself for a year at the Junior Academy for Applied Sciences, but he didn't like it very much!

Species: Human
Associates: Ezra Bridger, Jai Kell, Beck Ollet, Merei Spanjaf
Talents: Leadership, grav-ball, espionage

LIFE ON THE *GHOST*

The *Ghost* may belong to Hera, but the ship is a duralloy-plated home to the entire crew. The rebels experience a typical family life onboard: meals together, pranks, daily chores, starship maintenance... and not so typical life-threatening space battles!

Signature scrambling

The *Ghost* can jam Imperial scans or shroud itself with a false ship signature. Once, the rebels were even able to slip past an Imperial blockade, disguised as the freighter *Tontine* on its way back to Lothal from Boz Pity.

Mira and Ephraim Bridger's HoloNet transmitter

Diagnostic duties

Hera can't do everything herself, nor should she with a crew onboard. She assigns repair and maintenance duties to the others, but Zeb and Ezra are easily distracted by their constant squabbling. Chopper can fix just about anything on the ship, but he rarely does so without complaining!

A COMMUNAL SPACE

At the core of the ship is a social room, with ladders going up to the *Phantom* and dorsal turret. It is the ideal place for the rebels to tinker with equipment, discuss upcoming missions, or simply relax.

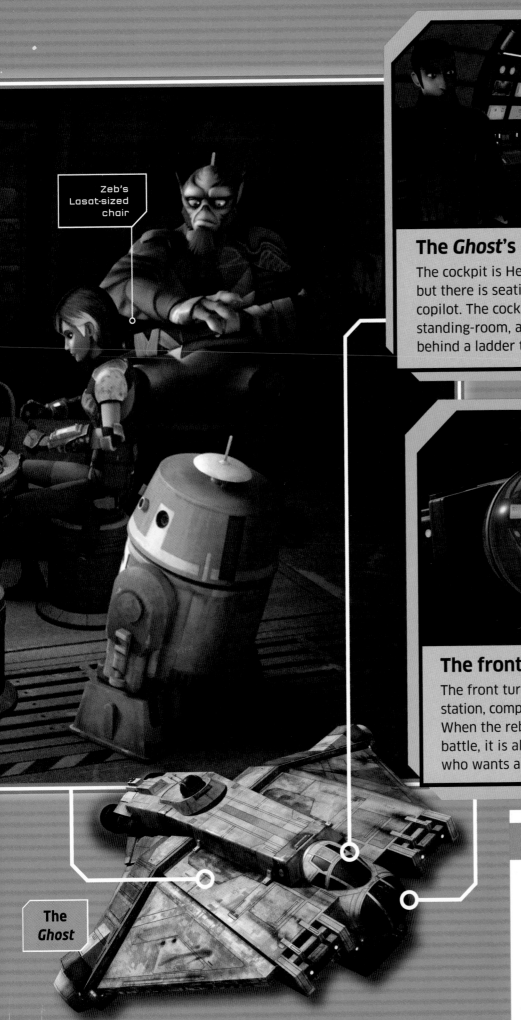

Zeb's
Lasat-sized
chair

The *Ghost*'s cockpit

The cockpit is Hera's personal workstation, but there is seating for four, including a copilot. The cockpit also has plenty of standing-room, and a plug-in port for Chopper, behind a ladder that leads to the front turret.

The front turret

The front turret is the ship's primary gunner station, complete with twin CEC laser cannons. When the rebels aren't engaged in a space battle, it is also the perfect place for anyone who wants a bit of peace and quiet.

The
Ghost

DATA FILE

MANUFACTURER: Corellian Engineering Corporation
CLASS: Modified VCX-100 light freighter
MAX SPEED: 1,025 kph (637 mph)

A FAST GETAWAY

Once the Imperial freighter is hit by the *Ghost*'s laser cannons, the kyber crystal onboard the freighter absorbs the energy and explodes. Hera jumps to lightspeed just in time!

Hera and Chopper fly the *Ghost*.

"We'll only get one shot at this!"

HERA SYNDULLA

Fighting for the crystals

Hera and Kanan locate the convoy of three Imperial freighters and their TIE fighter escorts. Kanan uses the Force to sense which ship carries the kyber crystal. After identifying it on the middle ship, Kanan lures the TIE fighters away in the *Phantom*, leaving Hera free to attack from the *Ghost*.

HERA'S SPACE BATTLE

Emperor Palpatine has been scouring the galaxy for giant kyber crystals, which he plans to use to build a powerful secret weapon. When Sabine sends the coordinates of an Imperial kyber crystal shipment, Kanan and Hera rush to destroy it.

Kanan pilots the *Phantom.*

DID YOU KNOW?

Famous Jedi Knight Anakin Skywalker and his Master Obi-Wan Kenobi once encountered an enormous green kyber crystal on Utapau.

HERA SYNDULLA

Hera is the daughter of the revolutionary hero, Cham Syndulla. He was a freedom-fighter during the Clone Wars, and inspired her to rebel against the Empire. She has traveled around the galaxy, looking for recruits to join the growing resistance.

Species: Twi'lek
Associates: The rebels, Fulcrum
Talents: Leadership, inspiring others, persuasion, piloting starships

One chance

The Imperials onboard the freighter ship realize that they are under attack, so they quickly decide to go into hyperspace. Hera has only a few seconds to hit her target before they escape with the kyber crystal. Thankfully, the most skilled pilot in the rebellion makes her shot count!

TIE FIGHTERS

The Empire's factories on Lothal produce a growing variety of TIE starfighters, including standard TIE fighters, cutting-edge TIE Advanced ships, and new, top-secret TIE bombers. The line of ships is the backbone of the Imperial Navy, and the scourge of the rebels and the underworld alike!

TERROR OF THE SKIES

TIE fighters scan the streets from above for any sign of rebel activity. Ships moving in and out of Lothal are closely inspected by passing TIEs, as the Imperials search for rebels, pirates, and smugglers. Suspicious vessels are vaporized!

Transparisteel viewport panels

Main support strut and energy collection hub

Formation flying

Without deflector shields, TIEs are vulnerable ships. They are strongest when attacking in larger numbers. The Inquisitor's TIE Advanced is surrounded by an escort of standard TIEs, which draw the *Ghost*'s laser fire away from him.

DID YOU KNOW?

The wealthy engineer Raith Sienar designed the original TIE starfighters. He drew influence from Kuat Systems Engineering's Jedi Interceptor.

A new paint job

Zeb and Ezra steal a TIE fighter from the town of Kothal. Although the two tell Kanan that they crashed the TIE, they secretly hide it instead. By the time the TIE actually comes in handy, Sabine has given it a custom paint job!

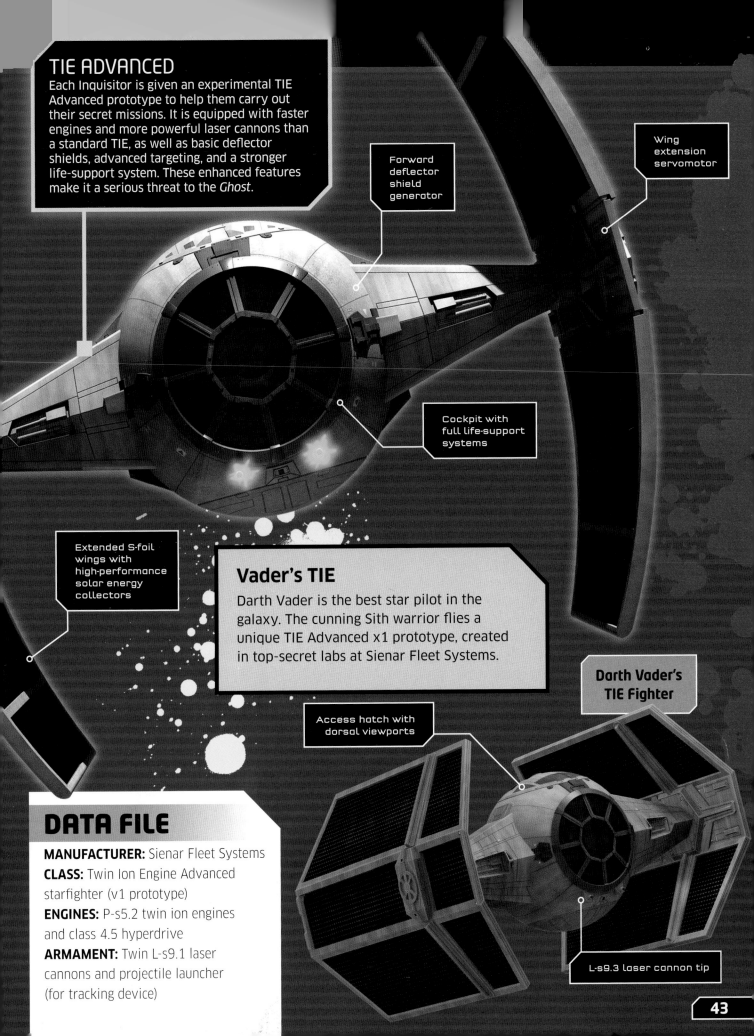

TIE ADVANCED

Each Inquisitor is given an experimental TIE Advanced prototype to help them carry out their secret missions. It is equipped with faster engines and more powerful laser cannons than a standard TIE, as well as basic deflector shields, advanced targeting, and a stronger life-support system. These enhanced features make it a serious threat to the *Ghost*.

Forward deflector shield generator

Wing extension servomotor

Cockpit with full life-support systems

Extended S-foil wings with high-performance solar energy collectors

Vader's TIE

Darth Vader is the best star pilot in the galaxy. The cunning Sith warrior flies a unique TIE Advanced x1 prototype, created in top-secret labs at Sienar Fleet Systems.

Darth Vader's TIE Fighter

Access hatch with dorsal viewports

DATA FILE

MANUFACTURER: Sienar Fleet Systems
CLASS: Twin Ion Engine Advanced starfighter (v1 prototype)
ENGINES: P-s5.2 twin ion engines and class 4.5 hyperdrive
ARMAMENT: Twin L-s9.1 laser cannons and projectile launcher (for tracking device)

L-s9.3 laser cannon tip

"Open Fire! Their shields will not hold indefinitely."

THE INQUISITOR

Flight from Lothal

The Inquisitor pursues the *Ghost*, leading a group of TIE fighters from his Advanced prototype.

ANSWERING FOR THEIR MISTAKES

The Inquisitor and Kallus stand to attention for the Grand Moff Tarkin. He has the power to make or break more than just their careers.

Working from the shadows

The Inquisitor has the authority to command uniformed officers and stormtroopers, but he often works alone. If he fails in his task, he must suffer the anger of his master, so he is determined to succeed.

AGENTS OF THE EMPIRE

Agent Kallus and the Inquisitor are both after the rebels, but their focus is different. As a member of the ISB, Kallus' duty is to arrest anyone involved in rebel activity. The Inquisitor, on the other hand, is only concerned with capturing the Jedi and their apprentices.

Calling for backup

Agent Kallus commands stormtroopers and has charge of his own Star Destroyer. When he discovers that Kanan is a Jedi, Kallus knows he is not qualified to deal with this threat, so he calls the Inquisitor in to assist.

DID YOU KNOW?

Both men fall outside the regular military channels. The Inquisitor answers to a Sith Lord, while Kallus is under the command of the ISB's Colonel Yularen.

Sharing the mission

The Inquisitor and Agent Kallus communicate with each other via a SoroSuub holopad. The two work in tandem on vital security operations. The Inquisitor is a well-trained pilot and often leads wings of TIE fighters, while Kallus manages ground support below.

FYRNOCK INFESTATION

As Hera and Sabine explore the base, passing wrecks of Republic gunships and starfighters, they realize that there are dangerous fyrnocks lurking in the dark!

Trust issues

Sabine hates having the truth kept from her. She tells Hera that being kept in the dark didn't work for her at the Academy and it won't work for her now. All Hera can do is assure Sabine that secrecy is the best way to protect the team.

KEPT IN THE DARK

Sabine is growing increasingly frustrated by Hera's secrecy. Now Fulcrum has arranged to meet Hera for a supply drop at an old Republic base called Fort Anaxes. Sabine insists on joining her so that she can meet this shadowy rebel contact.

SABINE WREN

Sabine was a cadet at the Imperial Academy on Mandalore. Sabine trusted the Empire blindly and never questioned orders. However, when she realized how evil the Empire was, she left her homeworld and joined the rebels.

Species: Human
Associates: The rebels
Talents: Designing weapons and explosives, acrobatics, art, speaking Shyriiwook

DID YOU KNOW?

Fort Anaxes is located on asteroid PM-1203. It was abandoned at the end of the Clone Wars. The rhydonium there was mined on remote worlds like Abafar.

They just keep coming!

Sabine and Hera use old canisters of explosive rhydonium against the attacking fyrnocks—but it isn't enough! They jump on top of the *Phantom*, desperately fighting off the predators. Fortunately, the *Ghost* arrives just in time to save them!

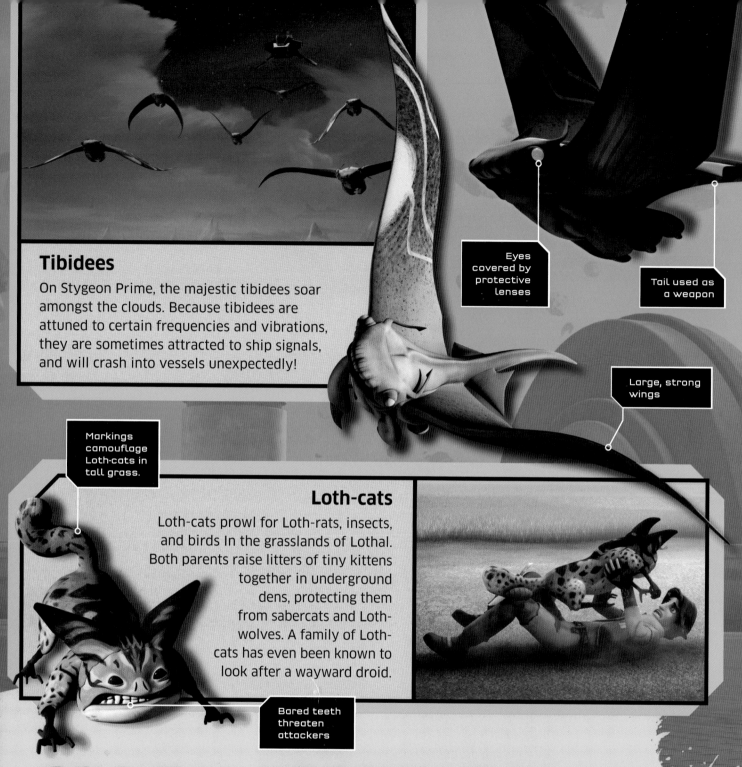

Tibidees

On Stygeon Prime, the majestic tibidees soar amongst the clouds. Because tibidees are attuned to certain frequencies and vibrations, they are sometimes attracted to ship signals, and will crash into vessels unexpectedly!

Eyes covered by protective lenses

Tail used as a weapon

Large, strong wings

Markings camouflage Loth-cats in tall grass.

Loth-cats

Loth-cats prowl for Loth-rats, insects, and birds In the grasslands of Lothal. Both parents raise litters of tiny kittens together in underground dens, protecting them from sabercats and Loth-wolves. A family of Loth-cats has even been known to look after a wayward droid.

Bared teeth threaten attackers

COSMIC CREATURES

The galaxy is full of animals that make their homes in the most unexpected places. This has led to the rebels encountering some very strange creatures on their adventures. Some have come in handy on missions, while others have gotten them into serious trouble!

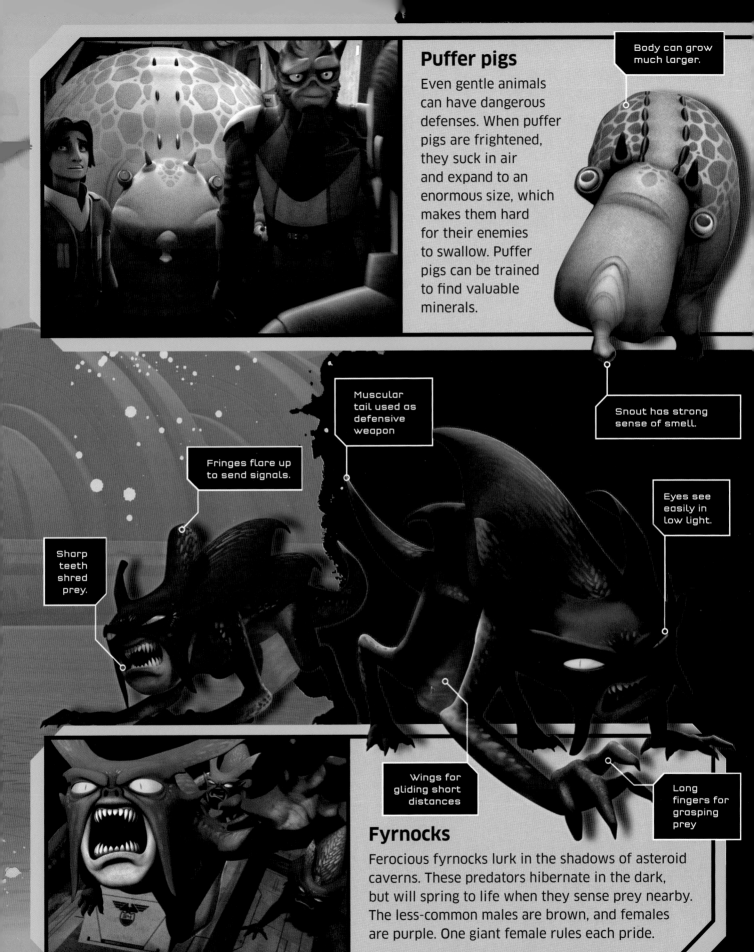

Puffer pigs

Even gentle animals can have dangerous defenses. When puffer pigs are frightened, they suck in air and expand to an enormous size, which makes them hard for their enemies to swallow. Puffer pigs can be trained to find valuable minerals.

Body can grow much larger.

Snout has strong sense of smell.

Muscular tail used as defensive weapon

Fringes flare up to send signals.

Eyes see easily in low light.

Sharp teeth shred prey.

Wings for gliding short distances

Long fingers for grasping prey

Fyrnocks

Ferocious fyrnocks lurk in the shadows of asteroid caverns. These predators hibernate in the dark, but will spring to life when they sense prey nearby. The less-common males are brown, and females are purple. One giant female rules each pride.

Sabine's helmet

A Nite Owl helmet is a symbol of Mandalorian strength and independence. Sabine's helmet includes a macrobinocular viewplate, holo-imager for capturing holograms, and a comlink synced with the *Ghost's* crew.

Targeting rangefinder

Engraved ancient Jedi designs

Kanan's holocron

Holocrons are rare and valuable devices used by both Jedi and evil Sith. They can store immense libraries of secret knowledge, displayed as holograms. Only a Force-user can open a holocron and activate the memory crystal at its core.

Macrobinoculars

Ezra uses an old pair of custom macrobinoculars, assembled from scrap parts made by Naescorcom, VidGraph, and Neuro-Saav. They provide high-resolution digital zoom, enhanced night-vision, video recording, and target ranging.

Power button

Audio waveform display

Transmitter

These antique devices are banned by the Empire. They are capable of broadcasting across the Imperial-controlled HoloNet when used with additional slicer gadgets, like computer spikes. They primarily broadcast audio, but they can also transmit holograms.

DID YOU KNOW?

During the Clone Wars, Sith Lord Darth Sidious hired bounty hunter Cad Bane to steal a Jedi holocron and kyber crystal containing a secret list of children with the Force.

GALACTIC GADGETS

The galaxy is filled with clever gadgets, from blasters and missiles, to lasers and droids. The Empire is well-equipped with the latest technology made by large companies, but the rebels arm themselves with many handy devices—some of which they have built or upgraded themselves!

High-definition holorecorder

Dianoga spy droid

Model 9D9-s54 Dianoga spy droids are made by the Imperial Department of Military Research. Their simple design is deceptive. These intelligent droids follow targets and record every move they make. They transmit their data back to the Empire over secure channels.

ID9 seeker droids

ID9 seeker droids were created by Arakyd Industries, which also makes viper probe droids and recon droids. These droids are a favorite companion of one of the Empire's Inquisitors. They seek out targets and then transmit data back to their master. They can also mimic sounds to lure their prey for an ambush. They are most deadly when working as a flock.

Optical sensor

EMPIRE DAY

Ezra Bridger was born on the day that the Empire was established. The annual Empire Day celebration makes Ezra sad as he remembers his missing parents. But when the Empire plans a parade to show off its new TIE Advanced, the rebels see an opportunity to strike!

BARON VALEN RUDOR

The arrogant Baron Rudor (code-name: LS-607) hails from the Core World of Corulag. He came to Lothal to be a test pilot for the Empire's experimental ships. He is an ace pilot, but he has terrible luck!

Species: Human
Associates: Commandant Aresko, Minister Tua, Agent Kallus, Yogar Lyste
Talents: Fast reflexes, piloting starfighters

The Imperials tumble off of the podium.

The perfect distraction

While Sabine distracts the Imperials with a colorful fireworks show, Kanan sneaks past a pair of clueless stormtroopers to plant a bomb on the Baron's TIE Advanced. When he gets caught, he plays dumb and is allowed to pass!

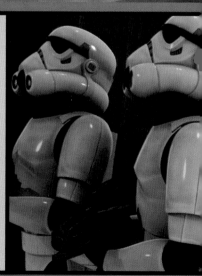

The bomb sends the TIE flying— without a pilot!

"Enjoy the celebration, citizen."
AGENT KALLUS

SPRING INTO ACTION

Kanan's bomb puts a sudden end to Empire Day festivities! The TIE Advanced is destroyed, and Kallus, Aresko, and the Inquisitor quickly search for the culprits.

Find those rebels!

The explosion takes the normally calm Minister Tua by surprise. She furiously orders a squad of stormtroopers after the rebels. Ezra leads Kanan and Sabine to his former home to hide, and there they discover an old friend of Ezra's parents...

Explosive impact

Sabine—very carefully—makes her own thermal detonators. They are useful for destroying Imperial vehicles and leaving stormtroopers stranded, while the rebels get away with Imperial property. The explosions can be powerful, so the rebels are quick to get out of the way!

BOOM
OR

Creative distraction

Sabine loves to combine her artistic talents with her knowledge of explosives. Beautiful fireworks shows can distract a large crowd with loud bangs and bright colors, while the rebels move behind the scenes.

Blocking the way

Thermal detonators are great for stalling Imperial reinforcements. From prison elevators to the Empire's bridges on Lothal, the damage stops stormtroopers from pursuing the rebels. Sabine is particularly fond of demolishing the Empire's landing fields in Capital City.

"Sabine, blow 'em up."

KANAN JARRUS

BUST!

Pulse detonations

The rebels use electromagnetic pulse emitters (EMPs) to disable ships of all sizes, from TIEs to Star Destroyers. They can also be used to leave stormtroopers in a daze! During the Clone Wars, rebels on Onderon used "droid popper" EMPs to disable battle droids.

The rebels use explosions for a variety of creative purposes. They are trying to save the galaxy—not destroy it—so the rebels carefully stick to strategic Imperial targets only.

Smokescreen

When the rebels are backed into a corner, a smoke bomb will impair the stormtroopers' vision and allow the rebels to escape. However, it can still be a risky move, because Imperials may fire blindly into the smoke.

TSEEBO

The Rodian Tseebo is an Imperial Information Office worker who has escaped and is on the run—along with top-secret information about the Empire! Finding him proves to be a painful blast from the past for Ezra, who must decide whether or not to help his old family friend.

SPECIAL EQUIPMENT:
Cyborg-Tech Headgear (Borg Construct Aj^2b)

SPECIES: Rodian
AGE: 38
HOMEWORLD: Lothal

Cyborg-Tech Headgear with wireless computer link

Full-spectrum holographic projector

Pads help Rodians climb through wetland vegetation

Imperial Information Office Technician's uniform

Wanted Rodian

The Empire blockades Lothal to prevent Tseebo from escaping with their secret information. They detain any Rodian that matches Tseebo's description, and the unlucky Tsoklo gets stopped by Imperial patrols time after time. Meanwhile, Tseebo manages to hide out under the protection of Ezra's friends.

DID YOU KNOW?

IIO workers wear cyborg brain implants, which allow their wearers t... effic...

ESCAPE THE EMPIRE

The rebels decide to help Tseebo escape from Lothal. Once he's onboard the *Ghost*, Tseebo alerts the crew that the Inquisitor is tracking their ship!

"Tseebo matters to you."

KANAN TO EZRA

Family friend

Tseebo was a friend of Ezra's parents, Ephraim and Mira Bridger, before they were taken by the Empire. Ezra thinks that Tseebo betrayed his parents, but Tseebo had joined the Imperial Information Office hoping to find out what happened to the Bridgers.

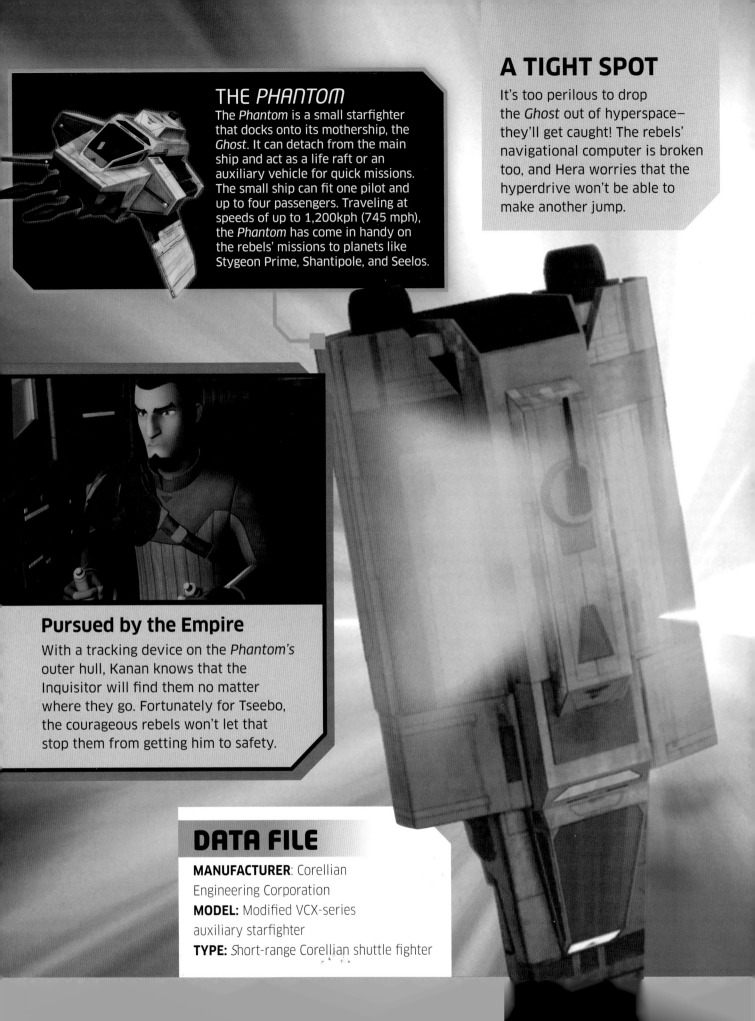

THE *PHANTOM*

The *Phantom* is a small starfighter that docks onto its mothership, the *Ghost*. It can detach from the main ship and act as a life raft or an auxiliary vehicle for quick missions. The small ship can fit one pilot and up to four passengers. Traveling at speeds of up to 1,200kph (745 mph), the *Phantom* has come in handy on the rebels' missions to planets like Stygeon Prime, Shantipole, and Seelos.

A TIGHT SPOT

It's too perilous to drop the *Ghost* out of hyperspace—they'll get caught! The rebels' navigational computer is broken too, and Hera worries that the hyperdrive won't be able to make another jump.

Pursued by the Empire

With a tracking device on the *Phantom's* outer hull, Kanan knows that the Inquisitor will find them no matter where they go. Fortunately for Tseebo, the courageous rebels won't let that stop them from getting him to safety.

DATA FILE

MANUFACTURER: Corellian Engineering Corporation
MODEL: Modified VCX-series auxiliary starfighter
TYPE: *S*hort-range Corellian shuttle fighter

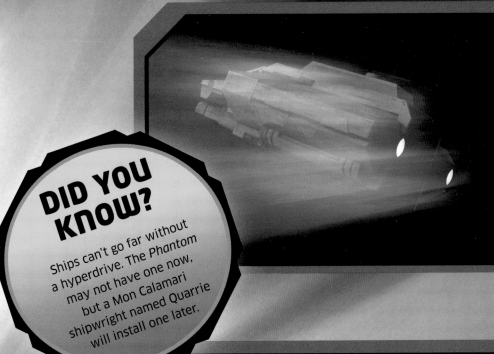

Two ships

Kanan and Ezra detach the *Phantom* from the *Ghost* and drop out of hyperspace. They will act as decoys, leading the Inquisitor away from the *Ghost* and giving the rebels time to take Tseebo as far away from the Imperials as possible.

DID YOU KNOW?

Ships can't go far without a hyperdrive. The *Phantom* may not have one now, but a Mon Calamari shipwright named Quarrie will install one later.

Risky maneuver

It is very dangerous for the *Phantom* to separate from the *Ghost* during lightspeed travel. Without its own hyperdrive, the *Phantom* could be torn apart as it tumbles between hyperspace and normal space. Although the ship spins out of control at first (and poor Ezra feels queasy), both vessels emerge safely!

HYPERSPACE CHASE

Tseebo and the rebels safely escape Lothal on the *Ghost*. However, they are pursued by Imperial Admiral Kassius Konstantine and the Inquisitor aboard the Star Destroyer *Relentless*. Now the rebels must meet with Fulcrum and safely deliver Tseebo to the Rebel Alliance before the Empire finds them!

EZRA FEELS THE DARK SIDE

The dark side is dangerously tempting. It offers immense power without the patience and selflessness required by the light side. As a Padawan, Ezra lacks self-control and focus, which makes him vulnerable to the dark side!

LOST IN FEAR

Ezra channels the dark side for the first time. His lack of experience with the Force means that he does not understand the havoc it can wreak.

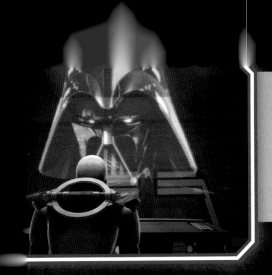

Seeking recruits

The Empire is concerned about Force-sensitive children. They plot to seek these "children of the Force" out and either turn them to the dark side or destroy them.

Dark side bargains

On Stygeon Prime, the Inquisitor makes a subtle offer to Ezra. He entices Ezra with a deal that could save Ezra's life... if he joins the Inquisitor on the dark side. Ezra, however, isn't interested!

Anger takes over

Ezra's anger and fear cause him to summon a fyrnock matriarch. Using the dark side leaves Ezra feeling cold and confused, and Kanan feeling worried for his Padawan.

Surviving a Sith Lord

After their first encounter with Darth Vader, Kanan explains to Ezra that their adversary is a Sith Lord, an evil being who uses the dark side. Kanan knows that they were lucky to survive!

LEADERS OF THE PACK

Protective instinct

The Jedi Knights were once the guardians of peace and justice throughout the galaxy. Kanan still feels a duty to protect the weak, as well as his family aboard the *Ghost*. He will do whatever it takes to keep the other rebels safe.

Unprotected shoulder

Like a family

Hera and Kanan stop life on the *Ghost* from getting too crazy! Kanan's authoritative nature keeps everyone in check, while Hera acts as the peacekeeper amongst the crew. They are always ready to offer advice to anyone who needs it.

"Kanan wanted to inspire people."

HERA SYNDULLA

Hera and Kanan first joined forces after meeting on the planet Gorse. Hera is smart and cautious, while Kanan is brave, but sometimes reckless. The two may have their differences, but together they make an unstoppable team.

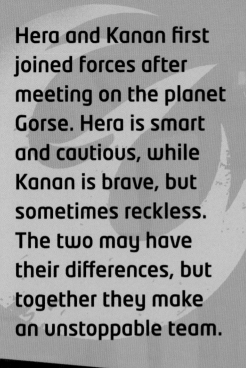

IN THE KNOW
Hera receives valuable information and mission details from a mysterious contact named Fulcrum. She doesn't tell any of the other rebels—even Kanan—that their crew is actually part of a much wider Rebel Alliance. Hera knows that hiding the truth will be safer for everyone.

Light armor for blaster fights

WHO'S IN CHARGE?
To outsiders—or even to some of the rebels themselves—it may seem like Kanan is the one in charge. He gives the crew their orders and is the front-man on missions, but it is Hera who decides most of their objectives.

DID YOU KNOW?
Kanan's codename is Spectre-1 and Hera's is Spectre-2. They are numbered so that Imperials will incorrectly assume Kanan is the leader.

THE JEDI TEMPLE

For thousands of years, the Jedi Order built temples on many worlds across the galaxy. Quiet locations were chosen, often because of the presence of rare kyber crystals. Kanan takes Ezra to the temple on Lothal, so that he can undergo a test.

Don't look. Listen.

The Jedi temple Kanan brings Ezra to is located in Lothal's highlands. The energy of the Force radiates from the central temple spire. Ezra listens to the secrets of the ruins as he presses his hands upon the icy stone. He senses that the temple will allow both him and Kanan to enter.

DID YOU KNOW?

Inside the temple, everything is not what it seems. Even Jedi can be fooled by powerful illusions—like the Jedi skeletons lying in wait for their Padawans!

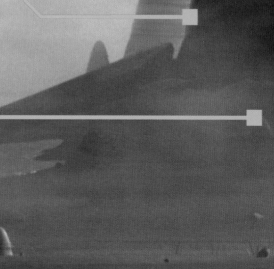

Signs of the Force

Around the temple base are mysterious concentric rings. It is thought that they trace the flow of the Force from the main spire. Among them are ancient symbols depicting the light and dark sides of the Force.

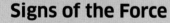

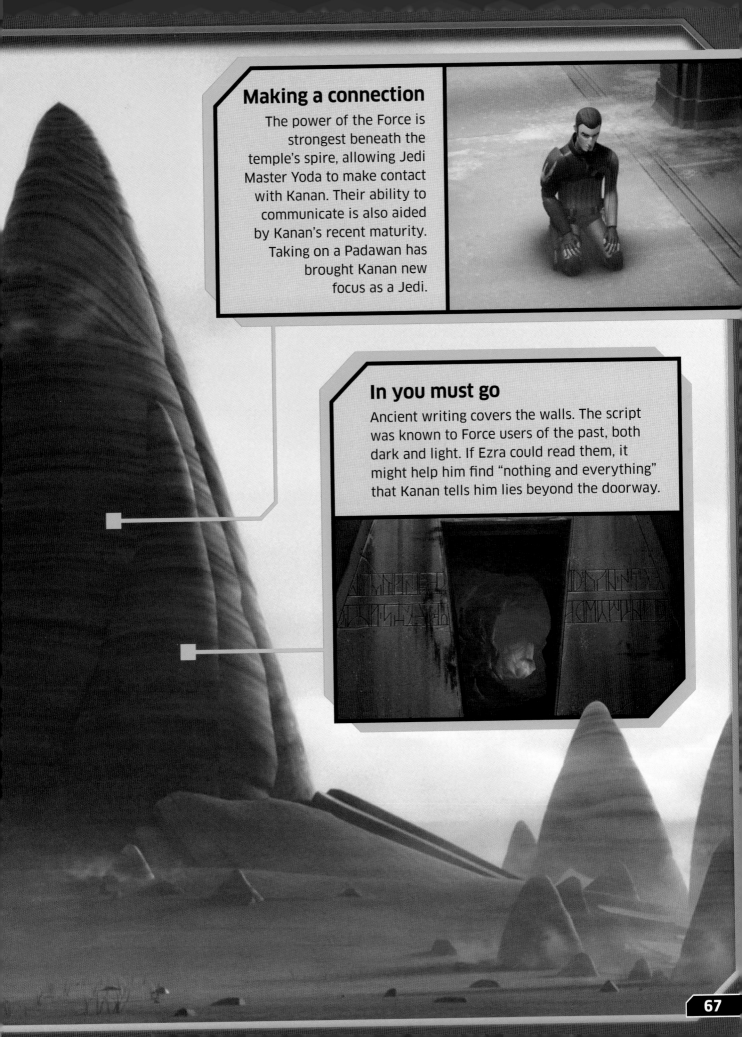

Making a connection

The power of the Force is strongest beneath the temple's spire, allowing Jedi Master Yoda to make contact with Kanan. Their ability to communicate is also aided by Kanan's recent maturity. Taking on a Padawan has brought Kanan new focus as a Jedi.

In you must go

Ancient writing covers the walls. The script was known to Force users of the past, both dark and light. If Ezra could read them, it might help him find "nothing and everything" that Kanan tells him lies beyond the doorway.

JEDI TEST

Ezra's brush with the dark side worries Kanan. He decides that the young Padawan must undergo a test. It will be very dangerous and Ezra must face all of his deepest fears. If he is strong enough to succeed, he will prove that he is truly meant to be a Jedi.

LEARNING CONTROL

Ezra ventures deep inside the temple and encounters a terrifying vision of the Inquisitor. Once Ezra remembers his training and admits his fears, then the Inquisitor has no power over him.

Mentor fears

Ezra is afraid of disappointing Kanan, and of losing him to the Inquisitor. Ezra must let go of these fears, and choose his own Jedi path, rather than simply trying to please Kanan.

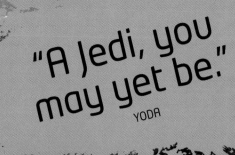

"A Jedi, you may yet be."

YODA

DID YOU KNOW?

A Jedi may undergo various trials in any place where the Force is strong and the dark side lingers. This can happen in ancient ruins or even natural settings.

Family fears

Ezra is afraid of rejection and of losing his new family. He fears being alone and is angry about losing his parents. Ezra learns to focus his emotions to protect those he loves—not seek revenge.

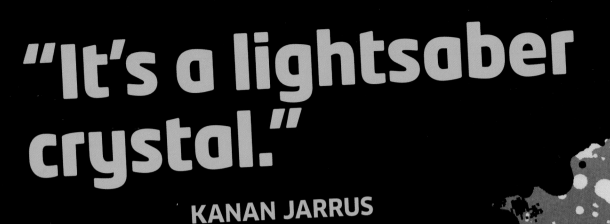

"It's a lightsaber crystal."

KANAN JARRUS

Ezra's reward

Ezra shows Kanan the kyber crystal he received from Yoda. It is one of his most important achievements as a Padawan.

Sith swordsmanship

Sith are aggressive by nature, and their goal is to conquer completely. They use fear and deception to unbalance their opponent first, before using their red lightsabers to attack and destroy. They show no mercy in combat, and take no prisoners.

Rebel Jedi tactics

Jedi are defensive fighters. They protect the weak and repel assaults. A true Jedi shows empathy for their opponent, so they may offer them a chance to surrender, or even retreat. However, when it comes to the Empire, the Jedi must now fight or die.

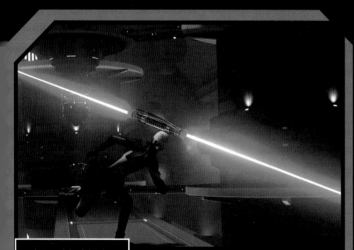

Double-blade rotation disk and hand guard

Deadly throw

Double-bladed Inquisitor lightsabers are all designed to rotate at dangerously high speeds. The circular handles are thrown spinning, and then recalled to their Master with the Force.

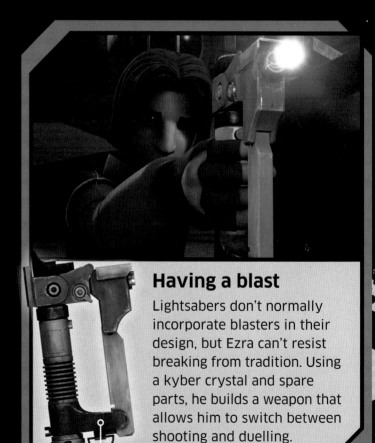

Having a blast

Lightsabers don't normally incorporate blasters in their design, but Ezra can't resist breaking from tradition. Using a kyber crystal and spare parts, he builds a weapon that allows him to switch between shooting and duelling.

Brace connects blaster module to lightsaber

Ahsoka's lightsabers

Clip attaches to belt

Handgrip ridges

Blade emitter shroud

White plasma blade

Power cell

TWO BLADES ARE BETTER THAN ONE

Ahsoka began using two lightsabers in combat while she was Anakin Skywalker's Jedi Padawan. She fights with an unusual reverse-grip, which makes defensive moves easier to perform.

After she left the Jedi Order, she constructed two new lightsabers with white blades. Her color choice shows that she is independent from the Jedi Order.

Blade projection plate

Blade length adjustment

Activator

DID YOU KNOW?

Jedi lightsabers are usually blue or green, while Sith lightsabers are always red. There was one known black Darksaber, last seen during the Clone Wars.

LIGHTSABER SKILLS

Force users have fought with lightsabers for thousands of years. Padawans learn lightsaber fighting forms from Jedi Knights and Masters while Inquisitors and assassins learn their skills from evil Sith Lords. The Sith now possess the secrets of the Jedi archives, so Jedi lightsaber combat is a dying art.

Mixed messages

Jho ignores the Imperial law that the HoloNet News should always be playing. The only time it plays is when a TIE pilot demands that Jho turn it on. The broadcast shows Governor Pryce's Empire Day Parade. Suddenly, the broadcast is interrupted by Senator Gall Trayvis, who urges viewers not to join in with the celebrations.

Phase 1 clone helmet

OLD JHO

Originally from Ithor, Jho was an early settler on Lothal. The village of Jhothal is named after him. Jho is a very friendly bar owner, but he keeps a hunting blaster under the counter in case of troublemakers.

Species: Ithorian

Associates: Kanan Jarrus and the rebels, Maketh Tua, Tsoklo

Talents: Gathering and sharing information, making connections

Word of warning

Jho is opposed to Imperial rule. He keeps his ears open for any information that could be useful to enemies of the Empire. When the rebels dock at his cantina, he often gives them tip-offs about possible jobs, as well as warnings about the Imperial activity that could put them in danger.

OLD JHO'S PIT STOP

This quaint bar in a remote settlement offers drinks, simple meals, and a discreet meeting place to smugglers, gamblers, and the occasional Imperial. The crew of the *Ghost* frequently visits the cantina and its friendly owner, Jho.

Repurposed moisture vaporator tanks

DID YOU KNOW?

Many of Jho's furnishings are made from repurposed goods, such as lamps built from pit droids and an overhead fan made out of a gunship engine.

Recycled relics

Jho decorates his bar with scavenged parts. The cantina owner claims that the Republic ship perched on the cantina's roof is the *Crumb Bomber*—the gunship that belonged to the famous Jedi Obi-Wan Kenobi during the Clone Wars. Other relics are scattered around the bar to remind patrons of the galaxy's wartime history.

LANDO CALRISSIAN

Lando is a smooth-talking con man who uses flattery to wiggle his way out of an endless string of sticky messes—all of his own making. His wrongdoings include smuggling, gambling, and outright theft! He comes to Lothal to try to strike it rich in an illegal mining scheme... if his luck holds out this time.

BlasTech Industries blaster pistol

Spacer's leather holster vest

Comlink

Gold dragon motif

SPECIAL EQUIPMENT: protocol droid, blaster pistol, mining facility, puffer pig

SPECIES: Human
AGE: 26

DATA FILE

Mind tricks

Lando tries to use his charm to get the crew on his side, playing them against each other to get what he wants. Little does he know, Chopper knows how to play the same game!

> # "I'm more of a... galactic entrepreneur."
> LANDO CALRISSIAN

Friends in low places

Hera and the crew aren't big fans of Lando, but he has his uses. They will call upon him for help when they need to sneak off of Lothal.

Puffer pig can smell precious minerals

DID YOU KNOW?

Lando's puffer pig plans won't be his only brush with mining. He will one day become Baron Administrator of a mining facility on Bespin.

RECURRING PROBLEM

When Lando drags the *Ghost* crew into his scam with Azmorigan, it has repercussions. He doesn't think through how it might affect them later.

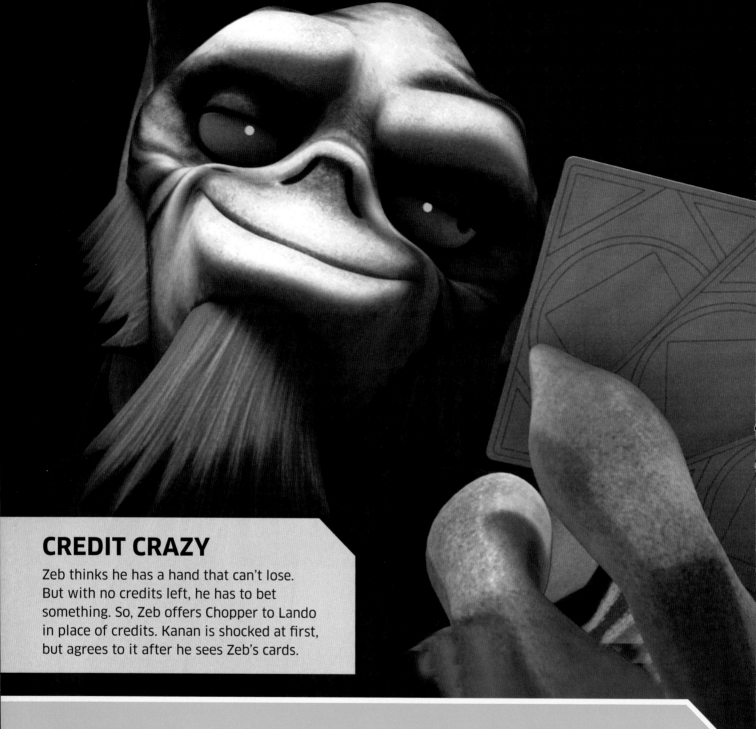

CREDIT CRAZY

Zeb thinks he has a hand that can't lose. But with no credits left, he has to bet something. So, Zeb offers Chopper to Lando in place of credits. Kanan is shocked at first, but agrees to it after he sees Zeb's cards.

CARD GAME CALAMITY!

Zeb gets carried away during a card game called sabacc, which he plays with Tsoklo and a stranger named Lando Calrissian at Old Jho's Pit Stop. Tsoklo drops out, but Zeb is so certain of victory that he bets something he probably shouldn't. Suddenly, the whole crew of the *Ghost* is caught up in Lando's scheme!

"See, I can't lose."

ZEB ORRELIOS

Chipper Chopper

No one expected Zeb to have a losing hand—except for Chopper! Zeb won't listen when he warns him to drop out, so the droid becomes Lando's prize. Chopper pretends to be a cheery servant to Lando to get back at Zeb.

Scheming stranger

Hera is furious when she learns that Chopper now belongs to Lando. But the scheming card player makes a deal with the crew of the *Ghost*: if they help him smuggle some cargo, he will return Chopper. It sounds simple enough...

DID YOU KNOW?

Zeb's cards are 15, -2, and 10—a great combination called "Pure Sabacc." But Lando's hand is the winner. His combination is called an "Idiot's Array."

PROPERTY OF AZMORIGAN

Smooth-talking Lando convinces the *Ghost's* crew to help him retrieve a puffer pig that he ordered from the crime lord Azmorigan. But just like all of Lando's schemes, the plan is not a simple one.

DO NOT DISTURB

Azmorigan is annoyed that Lando and the rebels have interrupted his mealtime. However, he is soon pacified by Hera's attentions. She waits for the right moment before knocking Azmorigan out and escaping.

AZMORIGAN

Large and lazy, Azmorigan is a slimy crime lord and slave owner from the planet Nar Shaddaa— a place that's well known for underworld activity. Azmorigan's impatience and hot temper haven't won him many friends.

Species: Jablogian
Associates: Henchmen; protocol droids; Cikatro Vizago; Lando Calrissian; the Rang Clan
Talents: Persistence, dirty dealings, deception

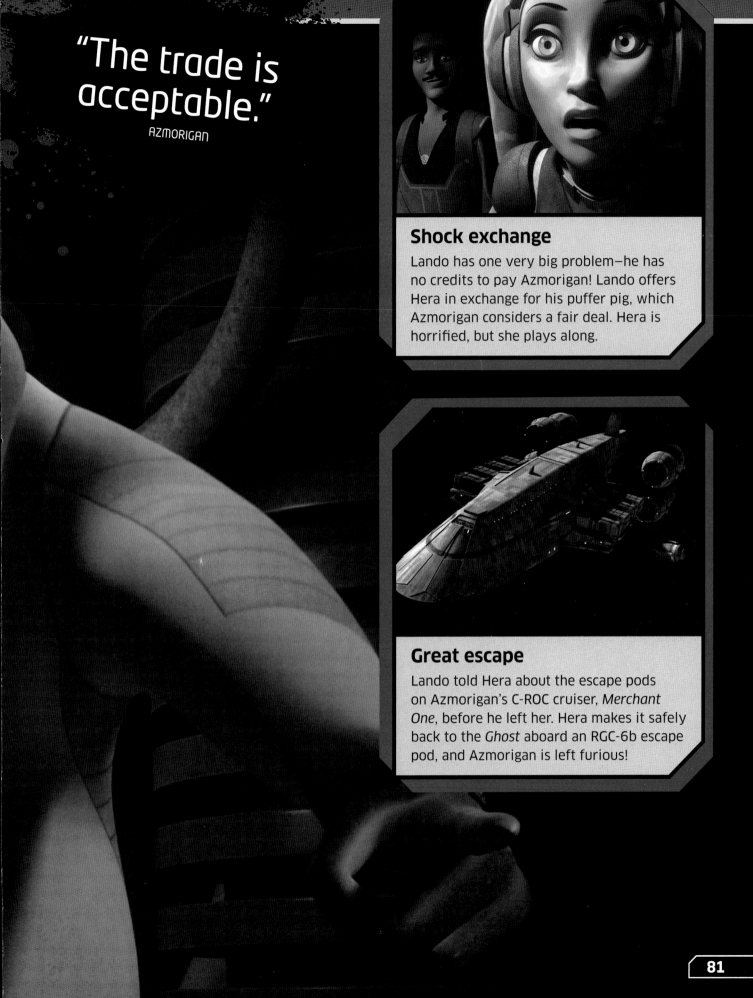

"The trade is acceptable."

AZMORIGAN

Shock exchange

Lando has one very big problem—he has no credits to pay Azmorigan! Lando offers Hera in exchange for his puffer pig, which Azmorigan considers a fair deal. Hera is horrified, but she plays along.

Great escape

Lando told Hera about the escape pods on Azmorigan's C-ROC cruiser, *Merchant One*, before he left her. Hera makes it safely back to the *Ghost* aboard an RGC-6b escape pod, and Azmorigan is left furious!

Revenge of Azmorigan

Azmorigan ambushes Lando and the rebels! Fortunately, a well-timed blast from Chopper gives the crew the upper hand.

Making impressions

Ezra makes an effort to impress Sabine—but it rarely works in his favor! No matter how hard he tries to look cool around her, she always seems to catch him being clumsy or doing something foolish.

EZRA AND SABINE

When Ezra first comes aboard the Ghost, Sabine ignores his attentions. Despite his attempts to impress her, she sees him as an annoying kid, or at best, a little brother. But as they spend time together, the awkwardness disappears and a strong friendship begins to grow.

SHARED BELIEFS

The two youngest members of the crew share similar ideas of right and wrong. When Ezra tells the rebels that he intends to disobey Hera to look for Kanan, Sabine is the first of the crew to side with him.

Getting protective

Ezra can't help feeling jealous of anyone who catches Sabine's attention. When the rebels first meet the charming Lando Calrissian, Sabine is impressed by his vast knowledge of art. Lando compliments Sabine on her own work, so Ezra is quick to point out that he appreciates her art, too!

What really matters

Sabine begins to warm up to Ezra, calling him by his own name rather than "kid." When she gives Ezra a holo image of his parents as a birthday present, Sabine shows how much she really cares for him.

A growing partnership

Sabine's dismissive attitude toward Ezra changes, as Ezra proves himself to be a loyal ally and brave rebel! Sabine can't help admiring him. She is happy to work alongside someone who is prepared to fight for what he believes in.

WORKING OUT THE CODE

Trayvis' broadcast contains a hidden message. Hera and Ezra figure out that he wishes to meet the rebels below the New Freedom mural in the Old Republic Senate building, today at sunset!

DID YOU KNOW?

HoloNet News is the Imperial news (or rather, propaganda) agency. It is overseen by the Minister of Information, Pollux Hax.

Ezra's vision of hope

Ezra has a vision about Trayvis, which leads him to believe that the senator knew and admired his parents. This makes him determined to help Trayvis. However, Kanan worries that Ezra's vision is clouded by emotion.

INTERRUPTED BROADCAST

Gall Trayvis hijacks the HoloNet to make a protest against the Empire. His speeches inspire the rebels, but the information that he broadcast about Luminara Unduli almost led to a disaster. Can the rebels really trust his word?

GALL TRAYVIS

Anchorman Alton Kastle's HoloNet broadcasts are often interrupted by Senator Gall Trayvis. He appears to live in hiding as an opposer of the Empire. Trayvis is an inspiration to many, including the crew of the *Ghost*.

Species: Human
Talents: Deceit, persuasion, making speeches
Equipment: Star Commuter Shuttle, protocol droids

Meeting the senator

The rebels find Trayvis waiting exactly where they thought he would be. Two senate RQ protocol droids guard him, armed with force pikes. Trayvis appears strangely oblivious to the possibility of his capture...

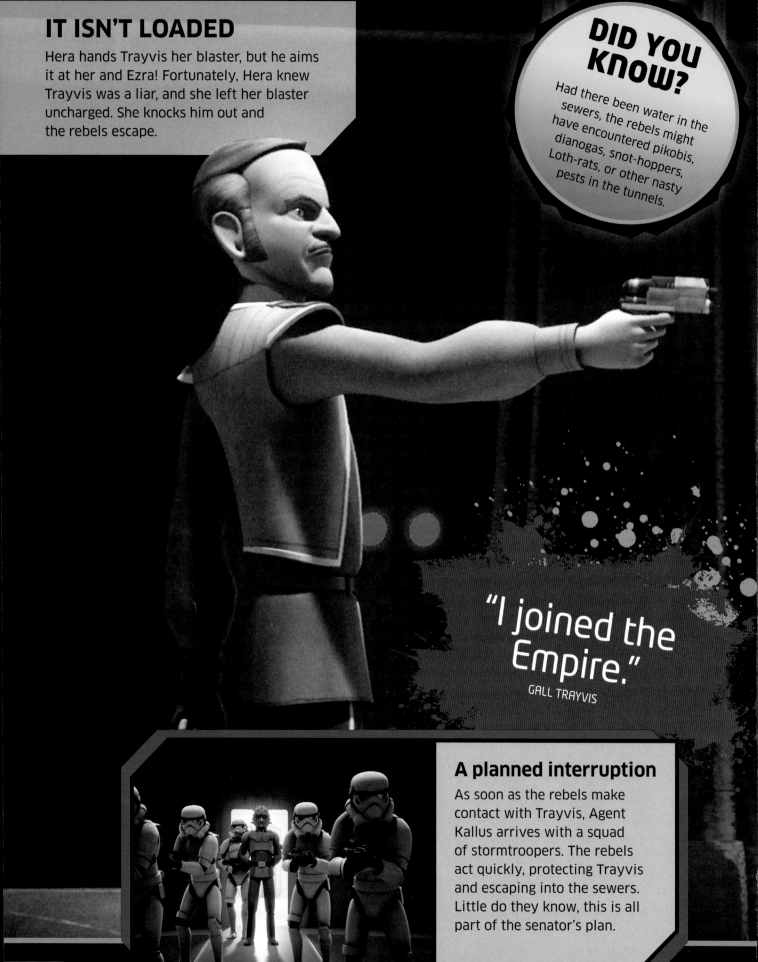

IT ISN'T LOADED

Hera hands Trayvis her blaster, but he aims it at her and Ezra! Fortunately, Hera knew Trayvis was a liar, and she left her blaster uncharged. She knocks him out and the rebels escape.

DID YOU KNOW?

Had there been water in the sewers, the rebels might have encountered pikobis, dianogas, snot-hoppers, Loth-rats, or other nasty pests in the tunnels.

"I joined the Empire."

GALL TRAYVIS

A planned interruption

As soon as the rebels make contact with Trayvis, Agent Kallus arrives with a squad of stormtroopers. The rebels act quickly, protecting Trayvis and escaping into the sewers. Little do they know, this is all part of the senator's plan.

Not what he seems

Hera grows increasingly suspicious of Trayvis. He seems to be in no hurry to escape, despite the danger and his questions are far too probing about their group's secrets. Trayvis seems very inexperienced for a supposed "rebel leader," living on the run!

DOUBLE AGENT

The rebels are shocked to learn that Gall Trayvis was secretly working for the Empire all along! His mission was to help the Imperials capture rebels by drawing them out into the open. However, the rebels don't fall for his crafty scheme.

"Move it, rebels!"
HERA SYNDULLA

Escape through the fan
Kanan uses the Force to stop the spinning fan. The rebels escape through it, leaving Kallus and the traitorous Trayvis behind.

Undercover missions

With a temporary paint job, Chopper blends in perfectly as an Imperial courier droid. He sneaks into restricted areas and gets access to top-secret information while wearing an Imperial Press Corps badge.

Rebel lookout

When the rebels need to sneak around on Imperial territory, Chopper makes a great guard. He's not easily distracted, and he has sensors to detect anyone who approaches—including stormtroopers.

Secret messenger

Just like many R-series astromechs, Chopper has a holoprojector. He can save 3D messages or even receive live transmissions over his antennae. This makes it easy for him to pass along messages from the rebels' friends.

Master of sabotage

Chopper has absolutely no regard for Imperial authority. As part of the *Ghost*'s crew, it's his duty to try to take down the Empire, so he's happy to blow a terminal to help disable an Imperial light cruiser!

A JOB FOR CHOPPER

Chopper is a plucky droid capable of tasks that others could never manage. His small size and determination help him slip in and out of tricky situations quickly. He may be a grumpy droid, but his sense of duty means his crew can always rely on him.

Expert mechanic

Chopper is equipped with a large selection of hidden gadgets which allow him to repair almost anything! His arc welder can cut through ship hulls, or seal ruptures and seams in most metal surfaces.

Attack droid

Chopper has no regard for other droids, at all! He especially dislikes bossy Imperial astro droids. Chopper doesn't hesitate to zap them with his electroshock prod if they get in his way!

Team prankster

Chopper likes to make his own entertainment, which often means teasing Ezra and Zeb! Whether collapsing Ezra's bunk bed on top of Zeb, prodding them both with electricity, or helping Zeb hurl milk canisters at Ezra, Chopper always manages to keep himself amused!

GRAND MOFF TARKIN

Wilhuff Tarkin is governor of the Outer Rim. Tarkin gained Chancellor Palpatine's favor as a captain, and later admiral, in the Grand Army of the Republic during the Clone Wars. He went on to become one of the most powerful—and ruthless—servants of the Emperor.

"Failure will have consequences."
GRAND MOFF TARKIN

Sharp but over-confident mind

Rank insignia plaque of a Grand Moff

Powerful signature posture

Code Cylinders

Officer's disc

SPECIAL EQUIPMENT:
Star Destroyer *Sovereign*

SPECIES: Human
AGE: 59
HOMEWORLD: Eriadu

DATA FILE

Cleaning up the mess

Aresko and Grint fail to stop the rebels during a theft of Imperial supplies, so Tarkin decides to make an example of them. He orders the Inquisitor to end the unfortunate officers' careers—and their lives!

DID YOU KNOW?

Tarkin oversees the ongoing secret construction of the Death Star. This moon-sized Imperial battle station will have the power to destroy entire planets.

TAKING CHARGE

The situation on Lothal is getting desperate. In Governor Pryce's absence, Minister Tua, Agent Kallus, and the Inquisitor have failed to stamp out Lothal's rebel cell. Tarkin intends to restore order!

Changing sides

Tarkin was once an ally of the Jedi during the Clone Wars. Tarkin and Jedi Knight Anakin Skywalker gained respect for each other when a team of Jedi rescued Tarkin from the Citadel prison.

Chain of command

The Inquisitor is directly accountable to Darth Vader, and Agent Kallus falls under the authority of the Imperial Security Bureau. Tarkin however, outranks and commands them all, answering only to the Emperor.

TIME TO SPEAK UP

When Gall Trayvis spreads damaging lies about the rebels on the HoloNet, Kanan decides to use the same HoloNet against the Empire. He and the rebels intend to hijack an Imperial broadcast and send out a message of their own!

An ambitious target

The Empire's main communications tower looms over the plains of Lothal. All transmissions on the planet move through this facility. If the Rebels can infiltrate it, then they can control all of the Empire's broadcasts.

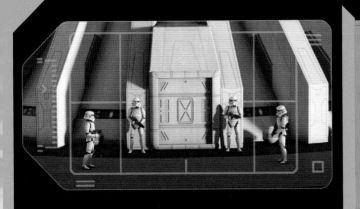

High security

The communications tower is guarded by three anti-ship turbolaser batteries. There are also four stormtroopers stationed at the door, and two more inside, monitoring the communications systems.

A simple solution

While the rebels look on, a troop transport drives past, dropping off an Imperial probe droid. The rebels fear being caught, so Ezra uses the Force to summon a Loth-cat and make it attack the droid!

DID YOU KNOW?

There are many types of probe droids. This dwarf probe droid is fitted with two blaster barrels, which it can fire with deadly accuracy.

THE PROBE DROID STRIKES BACK!

Kanan, Ezra, and Sabine perch on an archway overlooking the tower. Little do they know that the damaged droid can still transmit their location to Agent Kallus!

Seizing control

Chopper installs a Q-bazik computer spike into the tower's dataport hub. The spike allows him to hack into the Imperial communications system, so that the rebels can take control of it and make their own broadcast.

BREAKING AND ENTERING

Sabine races to the communications tower on her jumpspeeder. She tows a rhydonium canister behind her, and dismounts just before it explodes in glorious colors. The blast takes out the entire security patrol!

Once the rebels secure the communications tower, they have just three minutes to install their spike and get out—or so they think! Tarkin laid a trap for them. They accomplish their mission by getting their message out, but it comes at a great cost.

"We have to be ready to sacrifice for something bigger."

KANAN JARRUS

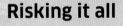

Risking it all

Kanan knows that Ezra is afraid of losing his new family. Before the mission, he tells Ezra that they must be willing to make sacrifices for their cause. They cannot let their fear stop them from standing up to the Empire.

KANAN'S SACRIFICE

The Imperials reach the communications tower before the rebels can escape. Kanan knows that his friends' only hope is if he can delay their enemies until Hera arrives with the *Phantom*. He sends the rebels up to the top of the tower and makes sure that the Imperials cannot follow.

BACK AND FORTH

The Inquisitor engages Kanan in a fierce duel. He sees that Kanan's fighting skill has improved, but he knows that it won't be enough. Ezra watches in distress from above, unable to help his Master.

"Spectre-2, get out of here!"

KANAN JARRUS

DID YOU KNOW?

Sacrificing oneself for others is a deed of a true Jedi. Kanan tells Ezra to run, just as his own Master, Depa Billaba, told him to run during Order 66.

Left behind

Kanan orders Hera to take the others and escape in the *Phantom*, and is taken prisoner by the triumphant Governor Tarkin. Kanan surrenders to his fate, safe in the knowledge that his friends escaped unharmed.

Interrogation

Kanan resists Imperial interrogation, refusing to give up information about the rebels. Tarkin knows that Kanan is no good to him dead, so he decides to transfer him to Mustafar—a place that never fails to make a Jedi talk.

Rebel inspiration
Ezra broadcasts a message of rebellion over the HoloNet. He is heard across Lothal, before Tarkin ends the transmission.

"Stand up together!"
EZRA BRIDGER

A fruitless effort

Sabine realizes that when Tarkin destroyed the Empire's communications tower, he also shut down Lothal's entire Imperial data network. After all their effort, their AT-DP has no connection to the system! Now they must try to escape— empty-handed and under fire!

Leave no droid behind!

Chopper may be stubborn, but deep in his circuits, he is a loyal droid. After the others evacuate, Chopper remains plugged into the AT-DP, still trying to access information about Kanan. Zeb has to run back to retrieve him.

AT-DP CHASE

The rebels hijack an Imperial walker patrolling the streets of Kothal. They hope to use the vehicle's connection to the Imperial network to find out where Kanan is being held prisoner. Unfortunately, their mission attracts some unwanted attention!

ALL TERRAIN DEFENSE PODS

The Empire uses lumbering AT-DPs to police the city streets, looking for any sign of suspicious activity. These walking tanks can crush almost any threat on Lothal... almost.

DATA FILE

MANUFACTURER: Kuat Drive Yards
CREW: 2 pilots (1 driver, 1 gunner)
MAXIMUM SPEED: 90kph (56mph)
POWER CELL: Rothana Heavy Engineering JJ-e5

CAUGHT IN THE CROSSFIRE

Two other AT-DPs chase the rebels through the market streets. As their own stolen walker runs on autopilot, Sabine, Zeb, and Ezra must balance on top of it and leap into the *Phantom*—without falling to the ground.

A DEAL WITH VIZAGO

Ezra and the rebels are desperate to find Kanan. When their search fails, Fulcrum orders Hera to give up on him. Ezra defies Hera by turning to Vizago for help. In exchange, he agrees to do any favor that the gangster might ask later.

USEFUL INFORMATION

As he agreed, Vizago tells Ezra that the Empire is using droid couriers to transport data from Capital City to a ship in orbit. This data may include Kanan's location.

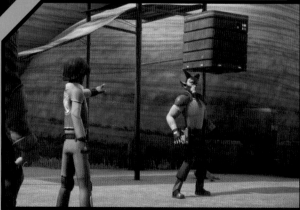

A shocking revelation

When Vizago ignores Ezra's request for information, Ezra tells him that he and Kanan are both Jedi. Vizago laughs at his claim—until Ezra uses the Force to lift a crate over Vizago's head! Now he really does have the crime boss's attention.

Ezra takes the lead

Hera is furious that Ezra disobeyed her direct order, putting all of their lives at risk. But even she feels conflicted about Fulcrum's instructions to abandon Kanan to the Empire. Ezra's plan to find him soon wins her over.

"You'll have a Jedi owing you a favor."

EZRA BRIDGER

CIKATRO VIZAGO

This native of Devaron is a powerful figure in the Lothal underworld. Vizago is always surrounded by a crew of IG-RM droids, who do all the heavy lifting and dirty work for his "Broken Horn" criminal operation.

Species: Devaronian

Associates: Azmorigan, Hondo Ohnaka, Lando Calrissian, Kanan Jarrus, Hera Syndulla, Ezra Bridger

Talents: Bargaining, illegal activities

Lothal

Located in the Lothal system of Lothal sector. This world of grasslands is important to the Empire for its natural resources.

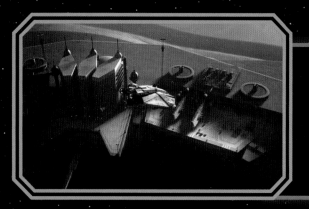

Kessel

Located in the Kessel system of Kessel sector. Wookies are made to work as slaves in Kessel's spice mines.

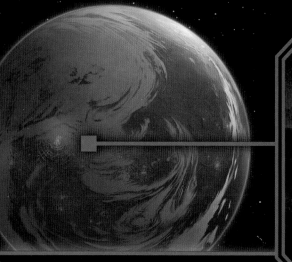

Garel

Located in the Garel system of Lothal sector. It is here that the rebels steal an Imperial shipment for Cikatro Vizago.

DID YOU KNOW?

Grand Moff Tarkin governs all of the planets in the Outer Rim for the Empire. However, he only travels there for emergencies.

WORLDS OF WOND

The Outer Rim may be far from the bright center of the but there are still many exotic worlds to visit. The reb journey from one planet to the next on their adventur all the while evading capture from the Empire!

Stygeon Prime

Located in the Stygeon syst
sector. Stygeon is a harsh w
seas. Palpatine's Spire prisc

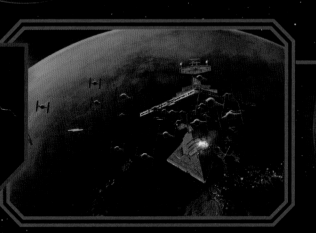

Mustafar

Located in the Mustafar
system of Atravis sector.
Tarkin takes Kanan to this
fiery world to question
him about the rebels.

Seelos

Located in the Seelos
system of Kwymar
sector. A dry, dusty
planet makes the
perfect hiding place
for the clones.

MUSTAFAR

The Emperor has long favored Mustafar as a place to conduct his darkest deeds in secret. Four Star Destroyers now orbit above this fiery world. Tarkin has brought Kanan here in the *Sovereign* to interrogate him, before his scheduled termination!

DID YOU KNOW?

Darth Vader was transformed by the fires of Mustafar. He underwent a total reconstruction while strapped to a table just like the one that held Kanan.

Making an entrance

The rebels' TIE fighter has been rigged with electromagnetic pulse (EMP) emitters. Chopper flies the TIE by remote onto Tarkin's Star Destroyer, the *Sovereign*, and Sabine detonates the EMP emitters. This disables the *Sovereign* as it hovers above Mustafar.

No time to lose

With the Imperials distracted (or knocked out) by the EMP blast, the rebels are able to sneak onboard the *Sovereign*. They must hurry though! The other Star Destroyers waste no time in sending reinforcements aboard *Sentinel*-class shuttles!

Reunited

While the other rebels fight off Imperials, Ezra sneaks through the air vents in search of Kanan. He finds his Master strapped to a torture table and quickly frees him. Now all they have to do is get off the ship!

SHOWDOWN

Kanan and Ezra face the Inquisitor in the engine room of Tarkin's Star Destroyer. In this final duel, Kanan is stronger in the Force than he has ever been before. The Inquisitor's defeat does not mean the end of the struggle for the Jedi and his Padawan...

"At last, a fight that might be worthy of my time."

THE INQUISITOR

Fallen in battle

The Inquisitor launches his spinning lightsaber at Ezra and knocks him off the walkway. Ezra survives the fall, but Kanan believes that he has lost his Padawan. Now that the worst has happened, he has nothing left to fear.

THE RISE OF A JEDI

Kanan begins the duel, wielding Ezra's lightsaber, alternating between blaster and lightsaber functions. Eager to help, Ezra uses the Force to take Kanan's stolen lightsaber from the Inquisitor.

Stronger than fear

Losing Ezra drives Kanan to destroy the Inquisitor for good. He engages the villain in a fierce duel, expertly wielding two lightsabers until he shatters the Inquisitor's double blade.

Haunting last words

The Inquisitor drops the pieces of his lightsaber into the reactor below, causing the ship's core to explode! Just before he falls to his end, he warns Kanan that "there are some things far more frightening than death."

Abandon ship!

Kanan and Ezra must find their own way off of Tarkin's doomed Star Destroyer. Now that the Inquisitor has been vanquished, he won't be flying his TIE fighter any more! Kanan and Ezra steal his ship and take off, just as the hangar bay explodes behind them.

HOT PURSUIT

Kanan and Ezra flee in the TIE Advanced, with Hera, Sabine, and Zeb behind them in the painted TIE. Unfortunately, a wing of enemy TIE fighters is following closely behind.

Nowhere to run

Hera, Zeb, and Sabine fly off the *Sovereign* aboard their TIE fighter, but they are shocked to discover that Chopper has disappeared with their Imperial freighter. This leaves them with no escape and vulnerable to Imperial pilots!

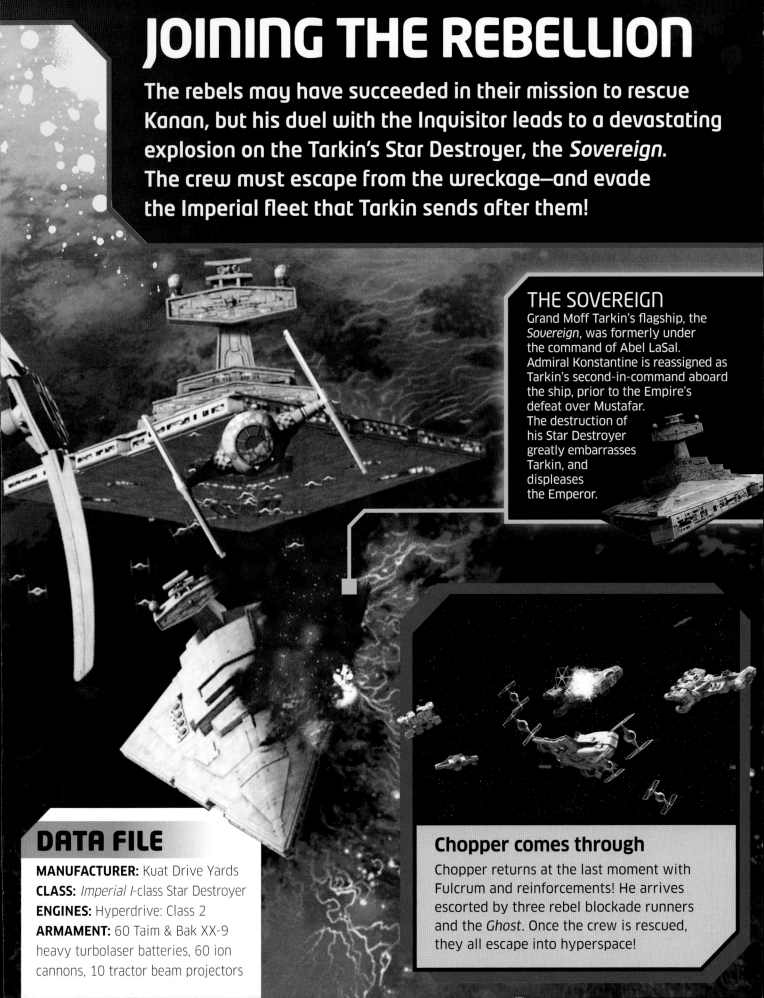

JOINING THE REBELLION

The rebels may have succeeded in their mission to rescue Kanan, but his duel with the Inquisitor leads to a devastating explosion on the Tarkin's Star Destroyer, the *Sovereign*. The crew must escape from the wreckage—and evade the Imperial fleet that Tarkin sends after them!

THE SOVEREIGN

Grand Moff Tarkin's flagship, the *Sovereign*, was formerly under the command of Abel LaSal. Admiral Konstantine is reassigned as Tarkin's second-in-command aboard the ship, prior to the Empire's defeat over Mustafar. The destruction of his Star Destroyer greatly embarrasses Tarkin, and displeases the Emperor.

DATA FILE

MANUFACTURER: Kuat Drive Yards
CLASS: *Imperial I*-class Star Destroyer
ENGINES: Hyperdrive: Class 2
ARMAMENT: 60 Taim & Bak XX-9 heavy turbolaser batteries, 60 ion cannons, 10 tractor beam projectors

Chopper comes through

Chopper returns at the last moment with Fulcrum and reinforcements! He arrives escorted by three rebel blockade runners and the *Ghost*. Once the crew is rescued, they all escape into hyperspace!

AHSOKA TANO

During the Clone Wars, Ahsoka was charged by Tarkin for a crime she didn't commit. The Jedi abandoned her—except for her Master, Anakin Skywalker. Although Ahsoka was proven innocent, she chose not to return to the Jedi. By doing so, she escaped the fate of the rest of the Jedi in Order 66—and has been fighting the Empire ever since.

Montrals sense movement

DNA determines Lekku colors

Protective metal gauntlets

Lightsaber hook

Semi-precious metal plating

Lightweight shin guard armor

SPECIAL EQUIPMENT:
Two lightsabers

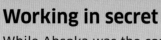

Working in secret

While Ahsoka was the contact for Hera and other rebel cells, she kept her identity secret by using the codename Fulcrum. However, the rebel protocol has changed. Now Vader also knows Ahsoka lives and he orders the Inquisitors to hunt her!

SPECIES: Togruta
AGE: 31
HOMEWORLD: Unknown

DATA FILE

REBEL COMMANDER

As a Jedi Commander during the Clone Wars, Ahsoka received an education in war tactics. Her experience is invaluable to the rebel cause.

DID YOU KNOW?

Ahsoka assisted one of the very first rebel cell groups—even before the rise of the Empire—as a Jedi adviser on Onderon during the Clone Wars.

Part of the team

Ahsoka plays an important role in the rebellion, serving as an advisor to Commander Sato and the *Ghost* crew. Due to her senior Jedi training and advanced combat skills, she is also a mentor to both Kanan and Ezra. She has other helpful friends to aid the rebels too.

One with the Force

During Vader's attack, Ahsoka and Kanan work together, reaching out with the Force to disrupt him. The attempt leaves Ahsoka open and vulnerable to her former Master, who senses her existence. Does Ahsoka sense something of Vader too?

COMMANDER SATO

Jun Sato coordinates with Ahsoka Tano and Bail Organa to lead a company of rebels from aboard his command ship. Though he networks with others who are sympathetic to the rebels, his resources are still limited.

Species: Human

Associates: Ahsoka Tano, Hera Syndulla, Bail Organa

Talents: Leadership, battle strategy, diplomacy, sabacc

DID YOU KNOW?

Before becoming Darth Vader, Anakin Skywalker once defended ships like Phoenix One during a space battle at Kaliida Shoals Medical Center.

BASE OF OPERATIONS

Ship movements are monitored on *Phoenix Base*'s bridge via a Plescinia Entertainments CS-Mark 9 holoprojector table. The 282.24m (932ft 6in) –long ship carries a crew of 900. When Vader destroys the ship, many escape aboard the ship's RGC-6b escape pods.

STRENGTH IN NUMBERS

No single ship in the rebel fleet poses a significant threat to the Imperial navy on its own. The relatively small rebel ships must stick together to survive!

Chopper works on repairs

Phoenix Base

Commander Sato's flagship is a repurposed Clone Wars-era *Pelta*-class medical frigate. It was manufactured by Kuat Drive Yards for the old Republic. *Phoenix Base* is equipped with turbolasers and point-defense laser cannons, but it is not powerful enough for a full-on assault.

THE REBEL COMMAND

Commander Sato's rebel collective has a small fleet of ships. Though his capital ship, *Phoenix Base*, is well-armored and heavily shielded, it is still not formidable enough in battle. Sato is forced to abandon ship when the rebel fleet is attacked by Darth Vader's TIE Advanced.

Rebel pilots

The pilots of Phoenix Squadron come from a variety of backgrounds. Some were members of the military, while others are defectors from Imperial academies. Some were even merchant freighter pilots with no prior combat training!

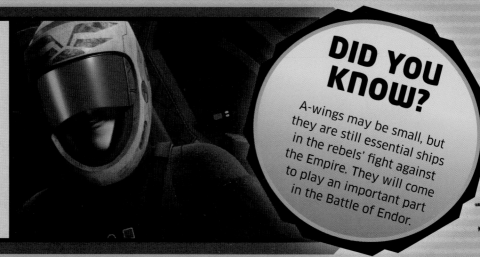

DID YOU KNOW?

A-wings may be small, but they are still essential ships in the rebels' fight against the Empire. They will come to play an important part in the Battle of Endor.

Into battle

Phoenix Base relies on its own small fleet of A-wings for protection. These high-speed ships lack room for an astromech co-pilot, which makes them especially challenging to fly. However, advanced shields and hyperdrives make them robust fighters.

DATA FILE

MANUFACTURER: *Kuat Systems Engineering*
CLASS: RZ-1 A-wing starfighter
ARMAMENT: 2 laser cannons, 2 projectile launchers

Borstel rotary laser cannon

A-wing starfighter

Deflector shield generator (internal)

Reinforced front wedge

Dymek HM-5 Concussion missile launcher (internal)

Sublight engines

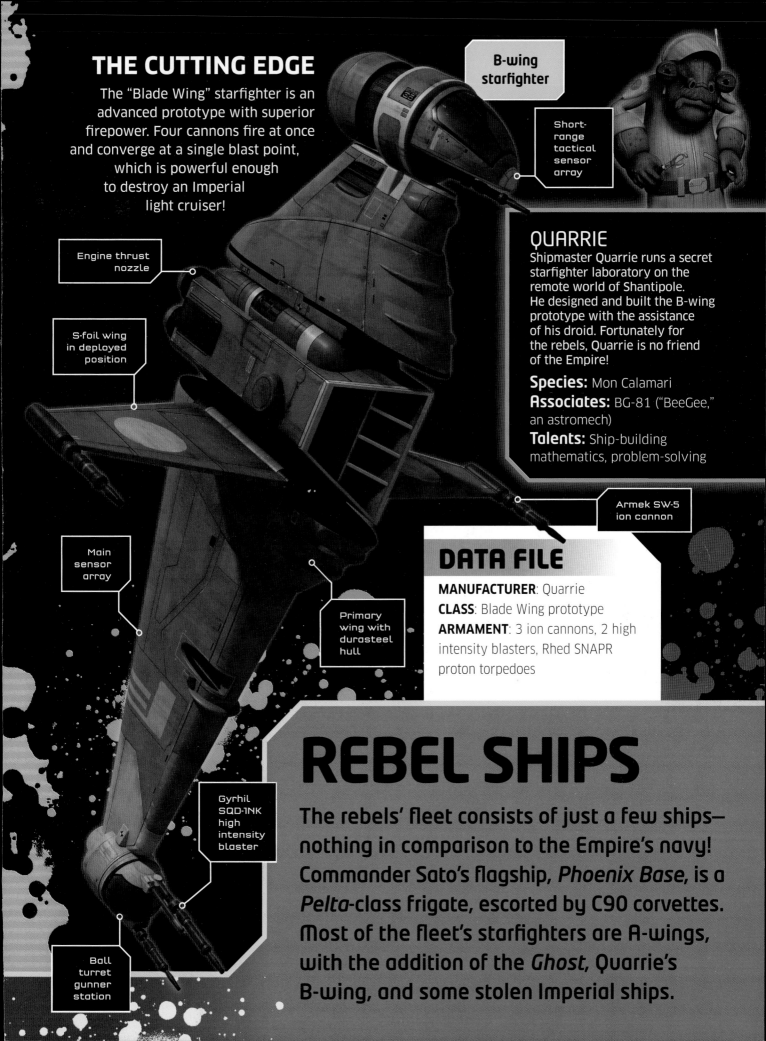

THE CUTTING EDGE

The "Blade Wing" starfighter is an advanced prototype with superior firepower. Four cannons fire at once and converge at a single blast point, which is powerful enough to destroy an Imperial light cruiser!

B-wing starfighter

Short-range tactical sensor array

Engine thrust nozzle

S-foil wing in deployed position

Main sensor array

Primary wing with durasteel hull

Gyrhil SQD-1NK high intensity blaster

Ball turret gunner station

Armek SW-5 ion cannon

QUARRIE

Shipmaster Quarrie runs a secret starfighter laboratory on the remote world of Shantipole. He designed and built the B-wing prototype with the assistance of his droid. Fortunately for the rebels, Quarrie is no friend of the Empire!

Species: Mon Calamari
Associates: BG-81 ("BeeGee," an astromech)
Talents: Ship-building mathematics, problem-solving

DATA FILE

MANUFACTURER: Quarrie
CLASS: Blade Wing prototype
ARMAMENT: 3 ion cannons, 2 high intensity blasters, Rhed SNAPR proton torpedoes

REBEL SHIPS

The rebels' fleet consists of just a few ships—nothing in comparison to the Empire's navy! Commander Sato's flagship, *Phoenix Base*, is a *Pelta*-class frigate, escorted by C90 corvettes. Most of the fleet's starfighters are A-wings, with the addition of the *Ghost*, Quarrie's B-wing, and some stolen Imperial ships.

A new threat
Darth Vader believes that the rebels' compassion is their weakness. He intends to use this against them.

"I want those rebels alive."
DARTH VADER

DARTH VADER

After Tarkin suffers a major defeat over Mustafar, the Emperor sends an "alternative solution." He commands his most trusted servant, Darth Vader, to break Lothal's rebels! Vader is a terrifying figure, whose most effective tactics are fear, deception, and brute force.

Vision enhancement receptor

Locking armored helmet

Speech projector and respiratory intake

Life support control chestplate

Heavy gauntlet covers robotic arm

DID YOU KNOW?

Darth Vader doesn't have a merciful bone in his body. His first duty was to wipe out the Jedi on Coruscant—including younglings!

Shin armor protects robotic legs

DATA FILE

SPECIAL EQUIPMENT: Sith lightsaber

SPECIES: Human cyborg

AGE: 38

HOMEWORLD: Tatooine

VADER'S SUIT

Darth Vader was badly injured by Jedi Master Obi-Wan Kenobi during their duel on Mustafar. He lost his lower left arm and both legs, broke several bones in his body, and was badly burned by the lava.

Palpatine gave Vader a full-body suit which provides him with essential life support. He needs to wear it at all times in order to stay alive.

Squeezing Lothal

Vader tells Agent Kallus of his plan to turn the people of Lothal against the rebels. He intends to make everyone believe that the rebels are dangerous criminals, whose actions are causing local people to suffer.

Dark Force user

As a Sith Lord, Darth Vader uses the dark side of the Force to perform advanced fighting moves, lift and control objects from a distance, sense the future, read minds, and choke his victims!

"Your 'Master' has deceived you..."

DARTH VADER

A LEAGUE OF HIS OWN

Darth Vader has the highest midi-chlorian count among Jedi or Sith—20,000+ per cell—which makes him very powerful. Even Kanan and Ezra together are not capable of defeating him!

Reluctant soldier

Kanan is hesitant to help Minister Tua but agrees, in part, because he wants to get back to Lothal. Kanan doesn't like being mixed up in Sato's larger rebel conflict. He prefers to simply help the people of Lothal and fight the Empire with the rest of his crew.

A bad feeling

The rebels were expecting Tua to come alone, so they are concerned when they see Agent Kallus through their macrobinoculars. They have no idea that Agent Kallus is acting on Vader's orders—this is all part of the Sith Lord's plan!

ASSASSINATION

Darth Vader has devised an elaborate scheme to turn the people of Lothal against the rebels—one that will cost Maketh Tua her life! Knowing that she is planning to defect from the Empire, Vader plans her assassination and intends to blame the rebels!

EXPLOSIVE END

To the rebels' horror, they are blown backwards as the ship explodes—with Tua inside! The Imperial HoloNet will broadcast the event, accusing the rebels of causing it!

Kanan in a stormtrooper disguise

"You did this!"

AGENT KALLUS

Futile escape

The rebels help Tua escape from her Imperial escort and run toward her *Sentinel*-class shuttle. The minister rushes aboard first, but Darth Vader has foreseen all of this. He has laid a trap for Tua and the rebels!

ATTACK OF THE SITH LORD!

After the assassination of Minister Tua, the rebels rush to get out of Lothal's Capital City. As they load a stolen shuttle, Kanan and Ezra feel a cold sensation... and turn to see the terrifying, shadowy figure of Darth Vader enter the hangar!

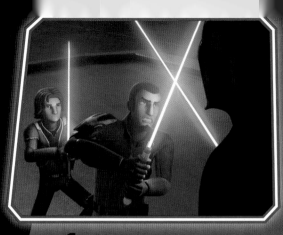

1 Vader draws his lightsaber and attacks Kanan and Ezra, without saying a word. Kanan tells Hera to leave!

2 Vader Force-pushes the Jedi and Padawan across the bay. Kanan scrambles back and clashes lightsabers with the Sith. However, Vader easily overpowers Kanan and grabs him by the arm.

3 Vader lifts Kanan by his arms, and then deactivates Kanan's lightsaber. Ezra watches him throw Kanan across the hangar as if he weighs nothing!

4 Vader turns his attention to Ezra. He makes Ezra lift his lightsaber and hold it to his own neck! He tells Ezra that he could never be strong enough to be a real Jedi.

5 Kanan lunges toward Vader, which causes the villain to lose his focus. Ezra drops to the ground. The three begin dueling again, but Vader slashes Kanan's arm with his lightsaber!

6 Sabine and Zeb watch from the sidelines as they exchange fire with Vader's stormtoopers. They throw a pair of magnetic thermal detonators at the nearby Imperial walkers, which causes a great explosion!

7 Kanan and Ezra take advantage of the explosive opportunity and Force-push Darth Vader beneath two Imperial walkers, just as they crash down on top of him in a smoldering heap!

8 Even this isn't enough to defeat the Sith Lord! Darth Vader uses the Force to lift the smoking wreckage off of him and toss it to the side! He continues his pursuit, barely harmed!

9 Sabine covers Ezra and Kanan as they rush to join the others on the shuttle. Vader deflects the rebels' blasts as the ship flies away. The rebels have escaped... this time.

A HEAVY BLOW

Some consider Darth Vader to be the best star pilot in the galaxy, and a cunning warrior. The pilots of Phoenix squadron are quickly and ruthlessly disintegrated by Vader.

The Empire strikes

Vader's TIE Advanced x1 has the Empire's latest starfighter technology. Vader is able to perform incredible feats with the ship, including flying backwards and in a spiral to avoid enemy fire. Only Hera and the *Ghost* are able to pose a threat to the Sith pilot.

"Your pilots are out-matched, Commander!"

HERA SYNDULLA

VADER FINDS THE FLEET

Darth Vader places a tracking device on the rebel's shuttle, before they escape from Lothal. Once they meet with the rebel fleet, the beacon is activated. Vader is swift to locate them and destroy their feeble ships.

Flagship destroyed

Vader strikes *Phoenix Base* with laser blasts! First he takes out the cruiser's shields, and then the hyperdrive. Sato refuses to abandon his flagship at first, but after it is continuously pounded, he agrees that they cannot stay onboard.

Darth Vader's TIE Advanced x1

A great disturbance

As the presence of Vader in the Force knocks Ahsoka unconscious, the situation feels hopeless, until Hera devises a clever plan. After ordering Chopper to divert all power to the hyperdrive, she leads Vader between two Imperial Star Destroyers. They accidentally capture him in their tractor beam, as she races away at light speed!

CLONE COMMANDERS

After their command ship is destroyed, the rebels must find a place to hide. Ahsoka suggests they contact an old friend—Captain Rex—who has a vast knowledge of the Outer Rim. She tells them to search for him on the planet Seelos.

DID YOU KNOW?

Clones' bodies age twice as fast as natural-born humans. This means that although the clones are technically 28, they have the bodies of 56 year-olds.

Commander Wolffe

Merr-Sonn RPS-6 rocket launcher

Trooper Gregor

Clone trooper gauntlet armor

Clone helmet with "Jaig Eyes"

Captain Rex

DATA FILE

SPECIES: Human clones

AGE: 28

HOMEWORLD: Kamino

SPECIAL EQUIPMENT: DC-17 pistols, blaster, rocket launcher

Clone War veterans

The Old Republic's army was comprised of clone soldiers. Chancellor Palpatine made sure they all had inhibitor chips in their brains, to control their behavior upon initiation of Order 66. When Rex learned this, he, Wolffe, and Gregor removed their chips.

Standard-issue DC-15 blaster

Wolffe in the flock

Wolffe has become a little bit crazy, perhaps due to lingering effects from his chip and difficult battle experiences. He knows that the Empire will not tolerate anyone who helps the Jedi, and worries about being punished for it.

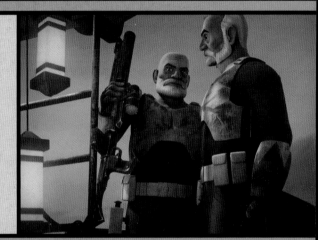

"A friend of hers is a friend of mine."

CAPTAIN REX

REPORTING FOR DUTY

The clones are wary of getting back into military service, especially fighting against the Empire. Nonetheless, Rex has a long history with Ahsoka, and eventually the rebels persuade him.

AT-TE CLONE TANK

The Republic's clone army once relied heavily on AT-TEs. The tanks have tough armor and can withstand many difficult environments, from asteroid surfaces to the hostile Geonosian plains. This durable vehicle serves as the perfect hunting lodge and retirement home for Rex, Gregor, and Wolffe.

DID YOU KNOW?

AT-TEs are easily modified for other uses. Elevators can be installed in the rear to unload cargo. AT-TEs can also serve as mobile command centers.

Boom and winch for hauling joopas

Outrigger towing boom with hook.

Finding Ahsoka's friend

It's not that difficult for the rebels to spot the clones' AT-TE on the salty plains of Seelos. There is nobody else around and nothing to see in any direction, except clouds of dust and distant blue mountains.

Home from home

The clones adapted their AT-TE into a more liveable home. Inside they've added sleeping bunks and a kitchen. Outside, they added railed walkways and ladders. Lanterns and bug catchers hang about—bugs are a great source of protein!

Widely spread feet for stable footing

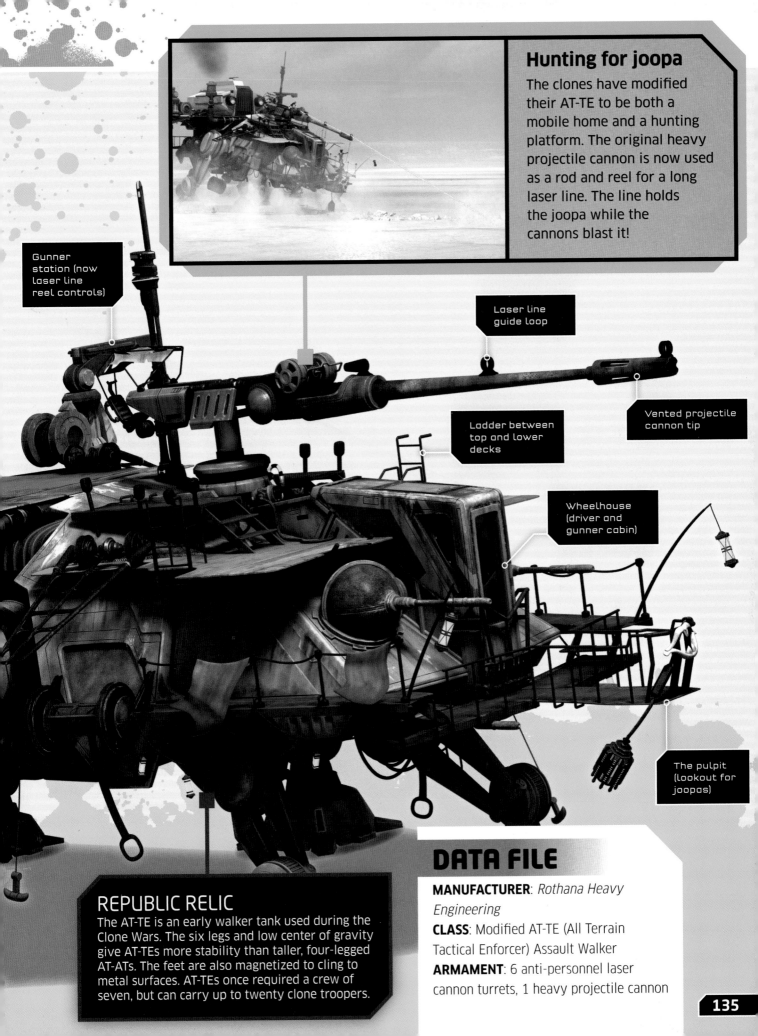

Hunting for joopa

The clones have modified their AT-TE to be both a mobile home and a hunting platform. The original heavy projectile cannon is now used as a rod and reel for a long laser line. The line holds the joopa while the cannons blast it!

Gunner station (now laser line reel controls)

Laser line guide loop

Ladder between top and lower decks

Vented projectile cannon tip

Wheelhouse (driver and gunner cabin)

The pulpit (lookout for joopas)

REPUBLIC RELIC

The AT-TE is an early walker tank used during the Clone Wars. The six legs and low center of gravity give AT-TEs more stability than taller, four-legged AT-ATs. The feet are also magnetized to cling to metal surfaces. AT-TEs once required a crew of seven, but can carry up to twenty clone troopers.

DATA FILE

MANUFACTURER: *Rothana Heavy Engineering*
CLASS: Modified AT-TE (All Terrain Tactical Enforcer) Assault Walker
ARMAMENT: 6 anti-personnel laser cannon turrets, 1 heavy projectile cannon

Multiple
bright
red eyes

Hunter or hunted?

Zeb walks ahead of the AT-TE, with the laser line tied to his waist. His bo-rifle is drawn, ready for a fight... but something isn't right. Suddenly Ezra figures out that Zeb is not hunting the joopa—he is being used as bait!

OPEN WIDE...

Ezra stands in awe of the mighty joopa! It bursts through the surface after he touches his electro-poles to the laser line, which leads into the monster's gut.

Bait

Only now do the other rebels realize what's going on. Kanan and Ezra shout out a warning to Zeb, but it's too late! Cracks appear under Zeb's feet and a long, slimy tongue wraps around him. Then it yanks him under the surface and into the belly of the beast!

THE JOOPA

Deep below the crust of Seelos lurks a worm-like beast called the joopa (or "big bongo"). Its crown is covered in bright red eyes. A joopa has hooked mouthparts but no actual teeth, so it swallows a person whole. The clones however, prefer to eat the joopa! Just one can feed them for a whole year!

> "Oh hunter, bait, it's… it's all the same."
>
> GREGOR

DID YOU KNOW?

Joopas enjoy the taste of Lasats, but a similar beast on Rishi Moon prefers the taste of clones! Like joopas, Rishi eels live underground but feed at the surface.

Electro-poles send bolts of energy

CATCHING A JOOPA

The clones strike a bargain with the rebels: If Zeb helps them catch a joopa, then the clones will trade some valuable information. However, the tasty joopa turns out to be a much more dangerous animal than the rebels were expecting!

ATTACK OF THE AT-ATS

Once an Imperial probe droid confirms the clones are helping the rebels, Agent Kallus sends a group of TIE fighters and AT-ATs to the surface of Seelos. This is the first time the clones have seen an AT-AT, let alone faced one in battle!

Republic vs. Empire

The clones refuse to surrender to the Empire! Instead, they unexpectedly charge their small, stocky AT-TE against the legs of the gangly AT-AT. Kallus is surprised—and shaken—by the daring move, but pounds the AT-TE with cannon fire!

ON THE RUN

Rex knows that the AT-TE is outmatched by three AT-ATs. He lures the AT-ATs toward a dust storm, where their scanners will malfunction. This gives the clones a tactical advantage!

Rebels to the rescue

Ezra and Kanan seize control of one of the AT-ATs by jumping on top of it and cutting through the hatch with their lightsabers. It's a risky move, but the rebels could never abandon an ally in their time of need.

DID YOU KNOW?

AT-ATs are the newest model in a long history of Republic and Imperial walkers. They will play important roles in many conflicts between rebels and the Empire.

"Will you look at the size of those things!"

GREGOR

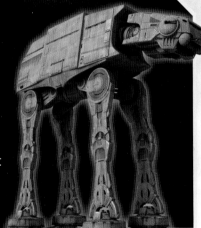

AT-AT WALKER

Despite its intimidating size, the AT-AT has some weaknesses. Although its hull has reinforced armor plating, the neck is a weak point and the four legs can have balancing problems.

DATA FILE

MANUFACTURER: Kuat Drive Yards
CLASS: Imperial All Terrain Armored Transport (AT-AT)
ARMAMENT: 2 heavy laser cannon turrets, 4 anti-personnel blasters, rear dorsal twin laser turret

Abandoned joopa is dead weight

Ithorians

Ithorians have two mouths; one on each side of their head. They cannot speak Basic (the most common language in the galaxy), so some wear translator devices on their heads to communicate.

Gotals

The horns of Gotals are sensitive to electromagnetic energy. This makes them irritable around droids and electronics.

Lasats

These honorable beings are now very rare. Lasats are tall and strong, but so is their smell! Their finger and toe pads help them climb great heights at high speeds.

Togrutas

Like Twi'leks, Togrutas are colorful and have lekku. Togrutas have tall, horn-like montrals on top of their heads, and some tattoo their faces.

Humans

Humans are a successful species living on many worlds across the galaxy. The Empire gives humans special treatment in the government and military.

AMAZING ALIENS

The life forms of the Outer Rim are as diverse as the planets on which they live. Lothal is home to many immigrant species. Many are friendly to the rebels, but some—particularly humans—offer

Weequays

On the desert planet of Sriluur, Weequays communicate by smell. They have thick, leathery skin and fringes on their jaws that grow as they age.

Wookiees

Tall, hairy Wookiees live in tree villages on Kashyyyk. Following the rise of the Empire, the Wookiees were forced to become slaves.

Aqualish

Amphibious Aqualish are native to the planet Ando, and have large eyes and mouth tusks. They can have nasty tempers and are often involved in illegal activities.

Rodians

Reptilian Rodians are originally from the swampy planet Rodia. They have a strong sense of smell and their big eyes help them see well in the dark.

Twi'leks

The Twi'leks of Ryloth have many different skin patterns and colors. They usually have two lekku (head-tails), but rarely have four. Females are famous for their beauty.

NEW THREATS

Darth Vader has succeeded in driving the rebels out of the Lothal system. The Emperor orders him to dispatch another Inquisitor to hunt them—and the apprentice of Anakin Skywalker—down. As the rebels face powerful new enemies, they will need to make allies who can aid them in their struggle against the Empire!